SUPERFOOD SOUPS

100 DELICIOUS, ENERGIZING &
PLANT-BASED RECIPES

SUPERFOOD
SOUPS

JULIE MORRIS

bestselling author of *Superfood Smoothies* & *Superfood Juices*

STERLING
New York

STERLING
New York

An Imprint of Sterling Publishing Co., Inc.
1166 Avenue of the Americas
New York, NY 10036

ISBN 978-1-4549-1947-6

Distributed in Canada by Sterling Publishing Co., Inc.
c/o Canadian Manda Group, 664 Annette Street
Toronto, Ontario, Canada M6S 2C8
Distributed in the United Kingdom by GMC Distribution Services
Castle Place, 166 High Street, Lewes, East Sussex, England BN7 1XU
Distributed in Australia by NewSouth Books
45 Beach Street, Coogee, NSW 2034, Australia

For information about custom editions, special sales, and
premium and corporate purchases, please contact Sterling Special Sales
at 800-805-5489 or specialsales@sterlingpublishing.com.

Manufactured in Canada

2 4 6 8 10 9 7 5 3 1

www.sterlingpublishing.com

CONTENTS

INTRODUCTION

"I love soup."

—Everyone

My long-time enchantment with cooking has lured new culinary books into my life ever since I learned how to read—my first cookbook being a tiny bound thing that told the tale of holiday candies with magical names like "divinity," next to pictures of children with impossibly round cheeks. I still have it. To this day, I excitedly whisk away a fresh cookbook in a manner that is indistinguishable from a squirrel with a big fancy nut, which I like to devour in bedtime-story manner at the end of a long day, until I fall asleep dreaming about delicious things. (No wonder I always wake up hungry in the morning.) I love recipes that evoke sizzling pans, aromatic sauces, careful drizzles, and desserts that make me quick to dismiss the confines of my favorite jeans. But, repeatedly, I find myself lingering longest on the soup pages. It's funny how even soups I've known forever, like a classic tomato-basil soup, can continue to sound (and taste!) so, so right.

There's a certain wave of sentimentality that comes with soup. For me, it's a feeling of home, being cared for, and a kind of calming energy, like that which comes with a simple, cozy candlelit evening. Even if it's far from a winter scene outside, I feel deeply nurtured when a steaming bowl of soup is lovingly set before me. I know I'm not alone, though. No, if there's one truth I've learned in my years of working as a chef, it's that *everyone loves soup.*

Ironically, it was while teaching a superfood smoothies class on a chilly Saturday in San Francisco that the importance of soups, in the context of a healthy lifestyle, really took center stage for me. A woman in the front row cleared her throat and, gripping her scarf as if to emphasize the temperature outside, asked me, "So, can you make hot smoothies?" As I was pouring a cup of ice into the blender, I couldn't help but chuckle at the unappetizing thought of gooey hot bananas and almond milk with some lumpy spinach, and quipped something along the lines of, "Well, I think that's just called a soup!" After the laughter died, the truth remained: in a way, a soup is almost the same as a warm, savory smoothie—a tasty amalgam of whole food ingredients, blended or chopped small, with condensed amounts of easy-to-eat nutrition.

Not another week went by that winter before the subject of warm smoothies came up again: this time it was suggested by a friend in Germany, who didn't want to even think about opening his freezer for frozen berries. And then, bizarrely, yet again—just days later, in an email—a reader requested recipes for savory smoothies. While I repurposed my "that's called a soup" joke again in reply, I couldn't shake the thought. What was going on here—was this an emerging trend? Was all this mention of warm smoothies and savory smoothies (aka soups) something new?

Of course not. In fact, if there's one recipe "trend" that's truly ancient, it's soup. Originally, making soup was a great way to preserve whatever raw foods were around by combining them with water, increasing the volume (thus satisfying more hungry stomachs), and thoroughly cooking them, so the ingredients would last longer. The ancestry of soup is as deep and diverse as food history gets: since we've had fire and a pot to cook with, I don't know of a single time in history when the popularity of soup has waned, traditionally whetting the appetites of everyone from peasants to kings.

Although many classic soups have a good foundation, I guess you could say I view them more opportunistically. The flexible recipe structure of soup provides an ideal format for easily heightening nutritional value in so many ways. With the addition of remedial superfoods, soups become more delicious than their traditional formulas, more vibrant, and—incomparably—more energizing and satisfying. The result is definitely not your grandma's soup (although I'm sure hers is very good!). The soup recipes in this book take full advantage of long-standing culinary practices, combined with nutrition knowledge from every corner of the globe.

When I first began writing this book, I had a ton of superfood soup ideas right away; but I also knew I had a lot of recipe testing ahead of me. So I did a little anecdotal field research first. "What's your most favorite soup?" I asked my mom, the mailman, and almost anyone else I bumped into. Though the answers differed wildly, I quickly noticed the *reaction* was always the same. A wide, almost childlike grin would spread over even the sternest face, and rather than simply naming a specific soup, she or he would eagerly tell me a full soup *story*: ingredients, method, heritage, family, and culinary details: "You take the onions and you don't chop them, you grate them. My grandfather, who is Russian—what a character he was!—taught me that, which is the traditional way. I like to add a little bit of garlic and fennel seeds too, but that's just my own twist." As I listened to one tale after another, I felt emotionally warmed by the astounding effect that just mentioning the *subject* of soup has on people, no matter who they are or where they come from. The connection to this profoundly nourishing food goes so much deeper than just a dinner solution; family recipes are cherished like precious heirlooms—knowledge that we yearn to pass down and share, and which connects all of us to the same place of mutual, in-the-know "yum." The other thing I learned? Talking "soup" will officially become my new icebreaker at parties from here on out.

Because, you see, *everyone loves soup.*

Wishing you endless happy spoonfuls,
Julie

PART ONE

THE RENAISSANCE OF SOUP

There is something profoundly instinctual about the comforting nourishment of soup. Just think about cupping a warm bowl, lacing your fingers around the spoon, and enjoying a soothing mouthful of good, earnest food that glides down your throat. Even a freshly baked chocolate chip cookie gets envious of something as powerful as that.

SOUPS: A POT FULL OF POTENTIAL

From the moment humans were able to procure a waterproof, fireproof container, we have been making soups and stews—our first culinary breakthrough, other than single-ingredient meals. And while putting the exact date on the true origin of soup is almost impossible, archeologists suggest we've been making the stuff for at least 25,000 years. Perhaps this is where our deep feeling of *yes* to soups comes from; why soups are instinctually recognized as "something good to eat." Soup is inexpensive, easy to make, flavorful, deeply satisfying, and overall a great way to use up whatever ingredients are around.

These are just a few of the benefits of making soup, and our generation is certainly not the first to know it. Ancient remedial recipes have been passed down, generation after generation, in all parts of the world, from the discovery of 2,400-year-old soup pots in ancient Chinese tombs, which tell the story of a culinary tradition cherished enough to be taken into the afterlife, to the traditional French restaurant (the epitome of haute cuisine), which began simply as a place to procure hot soups (*restaurant*, literally translated, means "to restore"). Indeed, there truly is nothing more restorative, revered, or more culturally impactful than a bowl of good soup.

Ah, but we are a creative culture, are we not? We've come a long way from eating grubs mashed with hot water. One look at molecular gastronomy (or just a tour of your local supermarket) will tell you that! In our quest for delicious flavors and textures, we've taken almost every edible ingredient we can find and transformed it through the art of cooking into something that is often more in line with a laboratory experiment than anything else. For example, we've created ingredients like dextrose (corn) and alginic acid (brown algae)—a deconstruction of natural foods to a point where they are largely unrecognizable. While not every food development is a bad one, there are growing concerns about the sheer quantity of highly processed ingredients that the average person is exposed to on a daily basis. Armed with this knowledge, the pendulum swing has already begun—back to some of our oldest culinary roots, in order to rediscover the original flavors and nutrition of our ancestors' most prized foods.

I cannot express how thrilled I am to see this changing tide in our approach to what we are eating. The revolution is here, my friend, even if you and I are still at the forefront. Smoothies, juices, superfoods, salads, foods with real *color*—naturally clean foods, whole foods, organic foods, biodynamic foods, local foods—all are part of an unabashed celebration of truly natural things that are fresh from the earth. At a time when our society is on the brink of a food crisis, in terms of our health, the conversation among consumers and chefs alike is shifting to a simple realization. The answer to achieving sustainable wellness has been in front of us this whole time: *real food*.

Celebrating this modern, holistic approach to food is the core mission of this book. The recipes capitalize on the true potential of soups to become an enticing route to everyday health. Thanks to their accommodating structure, homemade soups can be composed of 100 percent natural, best-ever ingredients—no fillers, additives, or refined sugar, *just* the good things! And in these recipes, we rely on the power of superfoods, which, you may know, are the most nutrient-dense, benefit-rich foods on the planet.

By incorporating these incredibly energizing foods with fresh, organic foods from your pantry, superfood soups take gratification to a new level—taking old classics (like Potato Leek) to new beneficial heights, as well as creating extraordinary new favorites (such as Split Pea & Hemp Seed). Even more exciting, these soups are delightfully simple to make, versatile, and fun to eat. You will be amazed how much goodness is packed into every pot!

So, in many ways, the soup movement is really just a matter of ancient knowledge coming full circle. We are going back to the basics by eating a diversity of unadulterated foods. But this time, we have the opportunity to incorporate some of the most nutritionally-dense foods from all over the world into our diet. We're entering a new era of cooking that is unlike anything we've ever known before, with food that has the power to make each of us, our families, and friends *physically* better as individuals, via each bite we take. This is transformative food that you can actually feel as it nourishes and sustains you. This is the renaissance of soup.

SUPERFOOD SOUP PRINCIPLES

Many a practiced chef will be quick to point out the basic principles of soup: a good broth, a little fat, some aromatics and bulk ingredients, seasoning du jour, and you have yourself a proper soup (we'll expand on this method in just a bit). While these are indeed classic components, the goal of *superfood* soups is to take this method a step further—cleaning up the ingredient set by using "best-of" choices and adding underused powerhouses for the greatest gain. The result is a river of deep nourishment: easily digestible amino acids, minerals, vitamins, antioxidants, and numerous nutritional compounds that leave us feeling like someone turned on the light bulb of well-being from within.

So, while an artistic, spontaneous, just-throw-it-in-the-pot flair is always relevant within the relaxed matters of making soup, superfood soups work within a few boundaries to ensure that they always err on the side of truly "good for you." Simmer by these "rules," so to speak, and enjoy a deeply nutritious culinary alchemy that makes comfort food live up to its name long after you've scraped the bowl clean.

1 **Lean on whole food, plant-based ingredients.**

There are so many different theories on nutrition, dietary dogmas, and the like, it's hard to keep up with them all. But there's one thing they *all* agree on: eat more plants. With each delicious bite, the recipes in this book will help you achieve your goals (and in some cases, even your doctor's orders) of consuming more vegetables, mineral-rich tubers, fiber-rich whole grains and legumes, and protein-packed seeds and nuts. This plant-based foundation allows for maximum uptake of nutrient-density (micronutrients per calorie), along with deeply cleansing, healing, and invigorating results.

2 **Keep it fresh.**

Fresh ingredients are almost always best! Grab your tote bag and pay a visit to your farmers market (or kick back in the produce section of your local store), for you will notice that the bulk of the ingredients in this book rely on foods in their natural state, with a limited dependency on things like canned ingredients. Fresh ingredients are the epitome of clean foods: they have no fillers, additives, sugars, preservatives, or the like, and they are nutritionally complete the way nature intended. You'll also find that they offer much more flavorful results.

3 **But also keep it practical (and read the labels).**

Lack the hours to make your own stock or slow-cook your own beans? I get it—we live in a busy world! Don't let that deter you from enjoying a freshly made soup. There are plenty of good ready-made ingredients on the shelves these days that are organic and whole-food based, and will cut down your preparation time. When shopping, rather than look at the label for nutrition facts, read the ingredients first (they tell the bigger story), and purchase the product that comes closest to something you might actually make at home (in other words, if the can of beans in your hand includes an ingredient you've never had in your kitchen, there's a good chance it doesn't belong there anyway). The recipes in this book are intended to bridge the gap between slow cooking and instant meals, creating approachable recipes, most of which can be made in an hour or less.

4 **Season soups consciously.**

Any chef knows that if their dish tastes flat, adding extra fat and salt will usually do the trick. While making your soups unbelievably delicious is the ultimate goal, there are many occasions where beginning with the conventional large amount of oil or steady stream of salt is largely unnecessary. While I am absolutely not against using either ingredient in moderation, we know far too well that using oil and salt without any reservation whatsoever has detrimental results over time (such as hypertension and excess body weight). As you continue to make superfood soup recipes of your own, I encourage you to be discriminating in your use of these ingredients, and follow the basic rule: start with less, and add more as needed. In the meantime, the recipes here are designed to achieve great results while conscientiously using minimum levels of fat and salt—but *yes*, you can always add more.

5 **Trust your instincts.**

Have you ever found yourself in the middle of summer thinking about or even craving a slice of pumpkin pie? Probably not! As organic beings, we are inherently wired to be in tune with our natural surroundings, and it's both wise and environmentally friendly (and more delicious) to eat with the seasons. You'll find certain soup recipes in this book that just seem to feel right or sound good, depending on the time of year. Trust yourself: your body is yearning for exactly what it needs! By taking advantage of in-season produce, you'll not only be able to obtain more flavorful ingredients, but in many cases you'll save money, too. (Ever bought a watermelon in the winter? You'd think it was filled with gold.)

6 **Never stop being a health opportunist.**

Superfoods, our nutrient-dense heroes, are what catapult each and every one of the soups in this book from healthy and nourishing to truly invigorating and healing, with long-lasting remedial benefits. Though some ingredients may appear to be used in small quantities, remember that this is the very nature of superfoods: small amounts = huge results. Because soups are such

flexible recipes, I encourage you to always look for "bonus" health opportunities with every recipe you make. Ask yourself—post it on your refrigerator if you have to—"What can I add to boost my health just a little bit more?" Throw in some baby spinach! Sneak in a pinch of super-food powder! Sprinkle chia seeds like they were celebratory confetti! Always look for ways to stash a little extra nutritional currency in your body's health bank account. It all adds up.

7 **Absolutely love every spoonful you eat.**

All the talk about nutrient density is for naught if the soups you make aren't a positive culinary experience—something that you truly *enjoy* eating. You'll find that each recipe in this book is carefully crafted to coax out a wide range of flavors and textures, because the happiness that comes with eating foods you love is a key component of health, too! While you may feel confident in making the recipes as I've written them, they are certainly not the law. Once you get a handle on how superfoods can be used, don't be afraid to customize and make every recipe your own masterpiece—I mean, isn't that precisely what we've been doing with soups for thousands of years anyway? So yes, scatter your overgrown garden chives on top, add your favorite spices, fold in grandma's kitchen secrets. Make your healthy lifestyle so delicious you can't help but crave it. Key words: *your* healthy lifestyle.

SOUP BASICS

Soups vary wildly in flavor, texture, and even the way they are served. Nevertheless, most soups follow a basic structure, which acts a bit like a formula: a little fat, aromatics, base ingredients, seasonings, liquid, and, finally, add-ins (including more seasoning—to taste, of course!). Once you've learned the basics of this formula (beginning on page 14), you will be able to customize and create infinite recipes of your own.

GOOD FATS

No, it's not an oxymoron: "good fats" really do exist. In fact, these quality, plant-based fats serve as a major source of energy, enhance cardiovascular health, and promote brain function (to name just a few of their important benefits). From a culinary standpoint, almost all soups need at least a little bit of fat for ease of cooking as well as balancing and deepening flavor. And for the recipes in this book, you'll be leaning, for the most part, on two sources of fat: coconut oil and olive oil. Coconut oil tastes more like butter than it does coconut, and it is a beneficial, cholesterol-free way to enrich heavier produce like roots and tubers. Heart-healthy olive oil offers a slightly fruity base that shines in recipes with a Mediterranean flair and those that feature fruits (like tomatoes) and warm-weather vegetables.

Although each of these oils has its nuances, they may be used interchangeably.

Aside from their use in sautéing foods, good fats can also be incorporated during or at the end of cooking to add body to a dish and improve mouthfeel. Including the aforementioned base oils, there are many soup-friendly sources of quality fats:

* Cooking oils, like olive and coconut
* Nuts (and creams made from nuts)
* Seeds
* Avocados
* Olives
* Flavored oils (such as sesame oil or truffle oil, usually added at the end of cooking)

AROMATICS

The alluring aroma of a chopped onion sizzling in a sauté pan is akin to announcing, "I'm cooking delicious food!" to everyone in the house. Hence, the term *aromatics*. As you might have noticed, if you've ever cooked soups from scratch, most start with the same cluster of ingredients, usually loosely oriented around a French mirepoix, or a mixture of chopped sautéed vegetables. A mirepoix ratio is usually composed of two parts onion, one part carrot, and one part celery, but you can add, substitute, and infinitely tweak the ingredients in this formula, as cooks from around the world have done for centuries.

Aromatics are the first ingredients that go into the pot when you start making a soup because they take the longest to cook down and influence the taste of the soup. Much like an ensemble cast in musical theatre, this group adds a vital background flavor, even if the individual ingredients are largely unnoticed. Common aromatic ingredients are:

* Onions (all colors/varieties)
* Leeks
* Celery
* Celeriac (celery root)
* Parsley root
* Carrots
* Parsnips
* Bell peppers
* Garlic
* Ginger
* Tomatoes

SEASONINGS

Seasoning really refers to anything with a strong flavor that's used to support, elevate, and add complexity to the base ingredients in a recipe, bringing out the best in them. Seasoning can be as simple as salt and pepper or as complex as a 20-spice mole, and it is highly dependent on personal taste as well as the nuances of other ingredients in a recipe. Seasonings are usually added during the first part of cooking, then again toward the end, to dial in flavor.

Any of these ingredients will add interesting notes (and hopefully harmony) to your soup:

* Salt and pepper
* Whole and ground spices
* Fresh and dried herbs
* Chili peppers and hot sauce
* Soy sauce and brines
* Nutritional yeast

BASE INGREDIENTS

Base ingredients form the core of a recipe—they are the stars of the show—and in this book, plants are the go-to superstars. Within this healthy realm, there are thousands of wildly different base ingredients to use, including (but certainly not limited to):

* Beans
* Legumes
* Grains and cereals

* Pseudo grains (grainlike seeds, such as quinoa)
* Squash and starchy vegetables
* Roots and tubers
* Leafy vegetables, and almost every other kind of vegetable you can imagine
* Fruits
* Nuts
* Seeds

LIQUIDS

A soup would just be a stir-fry without the addition of liquid! Adding liquid to soup is really where the magic happens—an intriguing osmosis between the characteristics of the solid ingredients and liquid occurs, concentrating flavor as the soup simmers. To create most soups, stock is used to infuse seasoning, but sometimes water is the only addition you need for more boldly aromatic recipes. And though making your own stock is best, in terms of taste as well as health benefits (page 57 shows you how to make superfood varieties), an organic boxed variety will do just fine at moments where time is of the essence. (Avoid stock bouillon cubes unless you feel confident about the ingredients—usually, they're mostly composed of concentrated salt and yeast, and light on other good ingredients.) Excitingly, you can really get creative with liquids for soup making. Here are some of the most commonly used options, some of which are even better when used together:

* Water (purified, of course!)
* Stocks/broths (homemade, as on page pages 56–73, or store bought)
* Nut milks/nut creams
* Tea
* Juice (especially vegetable juice)
* Wine (red and white)

ADD-INS

Making soup is like a classical piece of music in many ways. Take the famous "Hallelujah Chorus" by George F. Handel, for example. You've got about 4 minutes of feverish *hallelujah*s bouncing off a cascade of Latin—just like all the ingredients in a pot of soup, merrily cooking away. Then, there's the famous climax: the final, super slow *ha… le…lu…*. And that *lu* just seems to hang there, in suspension with its dissonance, in desperate need for closure, until *finally…*the *yahhhhhh* triumphantly kicks in. The importance of that climactic *yah* is equivalent to the final ingredients you add to a soup. The *yah* can be some extra seasoning, a little bit of acid (like vinegar or lemon juice), the touch of broth to loosen a thick stew, or a final dollop of cashew sour cream to top off and relax a spicy chili. The *yah* coaxes everything into a final state of harmony, and brings balance to a soup that's otherwise almost there. These are some of the most common add-ins to be used at the end of cooking:

* Lemon/lime juice
* Vinegar (all varieties)
* Salt and pepper
* Sweetener
* Extra broth/water
* Oil
* Nuts and seeds, nut butters, and nut creams
* Sauces and condiments
* Fresh herbs
* Delicate leafy greens
* Toppings/accoutrements (see page 200 for recipes and ideas)

BEANS: CANNED VERSUS FRESH

Add beans to a soup, and you've quickly got your-self a meal. Beans are an exceptional source of plant-based protein and heart-healthy soluble fiber.

Now, there are few foods on the planet that don't taste a million times (or at least a little) better when you make them *yourself*. But I'll be honest: this is usually not the case with beans. Unless you're adding lots of spice, basic home-cooked beans are pretty much on par with the store-bought, canned equivalent (or even, dare I say, sometimes not as good).

Canned beans have many advantages in soup making. First, they're fast and cut down on your cooking time by hours and hours (and is it not the nicest thing to be able to cook a soup in under an hour, instead of all day?). Second, canned beans always have the perfect consistency. Believe it or not, mastering perfectly cooked beans can be a surprisingly difficult task (they can be undercooked and hard or, conversely, exceed-ingly mushy). Last, most soup recipes only call for a relatively small quantity of beans—different varieties of them, too—not always enough to justify the hours it takes to make them from scratch.

A FEW TIPS ON BUYING CANNED BEANS

1. **Buy BPA-free.** Make sure the label on the can specifically states that the contents are BPA-free. BPA stands for Bisphenol-A, an industrial chemical found in some plastics and resins, and often used in the lining of food cans. Prolonged exposure to BPA has been linked to possible health effects to the brain, behavior, and prostate health of chil-dren. Researchers have found that BPA can leech into food from cans that are made with BPA. So, to be safe, choose BPA-free brands.

2. **Always go with salted beans.** Buy canned beans that are cooked with salt (and avoid unsalted varieties) for soup making. Beans require a tremendous amount of simmering time to pick up flavor from the liquid they're cooking in, so if you add unsalted cooked beans to your soup, your beans will remain disappointingly bland. Salted beans, on the other hand, will meld almost instantaneously with other flavors in a soup base. Normally, I recommend using low-sodium products, so that it's easier to control salt intake; however, beans are the exception.

3. **Avoid unnecessary preservatives.** The ingre-dient label on the can should read: "Beans, water, salt," or, preferably, "Organic beans, water, salt." That's all that the beans (and you!) need. (For brand recommendations, see the Ingredient Resources Guide on page 219.)

If you still wish to use up your dried bean collection, I applaud your valor, and you'll likely save a little money as a reward for your efforts! For your convenience, here's a reference chart with cooking times for the different varieties of beans used in this book. Simply use 1½ cups of homemade cooked beans for every 15-ounce can that a recipe calls for, and vice versa.

HOW TO COOK BEANS

First, sort through the dry beans to remove any pebbles or debris. Next, soak the beans in water overnight, using a bean to water ratio of 1:4. (Alternately, you can use the quick-soak method by bringing the water and beans to a boil in a pot, simmering them for 2 minutes, and then letting the pot stand, off the heat, for 1 hour.) Rinse soaked beans very well, and then simmer them in a heavy-bottomed pot with fresh water and a little salt. Use the table, above, to determine the cooking time for the type of beans you are using. Check for doneness at the beginning of the lower cooking time.

1 cup dry beans = 3 cups cooked beans		
NAME	**DESCRIPTION**	**COOKING TIME**
Black beans	Medium size. Black exterior with light, creamy interior.	1–1½ hours
Cannellini (Italian kidney beans)	Medium size. White and kidney shaped with nutty flavor.	1–1½ hours
Garbanzo beans (chickpeas)	Medium size. Beige with rounded shape; nutty flavor.	2–3 hours
Kidney beans	Large size. Reddish color and kidney shaped; strong bean flavor.	1–2 hours
Navy beans	Small size. White with oval shape; slightly sweet, creamy flavor.	1–2 hours
Pinto beans	Medium-large size. Brownish-beige color with pronounced bean flavor.	1–2 hours
Soybeans	Small size. Round shape and black, green, red, or yellow in color. Buttery flavor.	3–4 hours
White beans (great northern)	Large size. White and oval shaped. Mild flavor.	1–2 hours

Note: Black-eyed peas, split peas, and all lentil varieties cook relatively quickly and do not require a presoak, which is why they are used in dry form in the recipes in this book.

COMPOSING YOUR SOUP

One of the many things I love about soups and stews is that a high level of culinary skill is not necessarily a prerequisite. You'll find that top chefs everywhere in the world offer truly complex masterpieces, but at the end of the day, your dad's famous chili is pretty amazingly delicious, too. Given all the different kinds of soup that one can make, it's understandable that methods may vary. Nevertheless, there is a basic blueprint for making soups. Once you feel comfortable using it, as you make the recipes in this book, you can follow the same guidelines to create your own remarkable soup compositions.

Fats: A little oil goes in first, usually in a heavy-bottomed pot over medium heat, to make sure ingredients don't stick and to help with caramelizing (browning). Make sure the oil gets nice and hot (but never smokes)—the first ingredients should sizzle excitedly as soon as they hit the pan.

Aromatics: Whether you're using a classic mirepoix—finely diced onions, carrots, and celery—or a mixture of other base vegetables, aromatics always go to the front of the line when it comes to making soups, as they take the longest time to cook (and are difficult to overcook) and offer supportive flavors to other ingredients. Aromatics are usually cooked anywhere from 2 to 10 minutes.

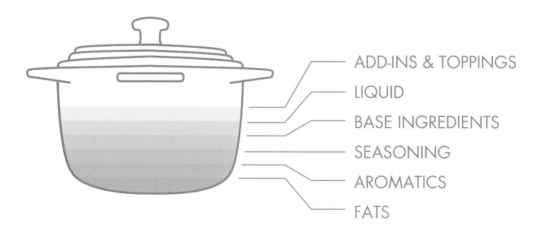

ADD-INS & TOPPINGS

LIQUID

BASE INGREDIENTS

SEASONING

AROMATICS

FATS

Seasoning: A little bit of seasoning—like salt, pepper, and dried spices—goes in next, to ensure it has plenty of time to bloom in the soup. Use a light hand with salt and pepper initially, as you can adjust the amount of each while the soup is cooking and after it is finished.

Base Ingredients: Dried rice, beans, legumes, hearty vegetables (such as potatoes and cauliflower), and heat-safe superfoods like goji berries get stirred in next. These ingredients take a little longer to cook through or release flavor, but they have a point where they are considered done. Cook until the ingredient with the longest cooking time is tender (or you can also add ingredients in stages to control the texture).

Liquid: Water, stock, wine, or any other cooking liquid of choice is added to soften the vegetables.

Even if the pot is covered, much of the liquid will be absorbed or evaporate. First, bring the cooking liquid to a boil on high heat, and then lower it to allow the liquid to gently simmer. Simmering time will depend upon the size and type of base ingredients used.

Add-ins: At the very end of cooking, add ingredients that are sensitive to or change with heat, including acids like lemon and lime juice, vinegar, milk, leafy greens, textural superfoods such as chia seeds, and delicate fresh herbs. Adjust the seasonings once again.

Toppings: Sauces like pesto, creams, toasted seeds, and additional chopped fresh herbs (such as chives, parsley, and dill) are usually added after the soup has been ladled into serving bowls.

TOOLS

Soups are refreshingly minimalistic when it comes to tools. To begin with, you'll need the basics: a big, heavy-bottomed pot, a good knife, and a trusty wooden spoon. For the pot, a stainless steel or copper pot is perfect. You can also use a Dutch oven (an enamel-coated cast iron pot with super thick walls), but this heavy beast won't offer any particular advantages over a regular pot for the kinds of soups you'll be making from this book. As far as size goes, a 6–8 quart pot is best (err on the side of larger if you're unsure).

A good knife will make all the difference in your soup making. Soups do require a little bit of prep work—light chopping—and your knife's quality and sharpness can either make this process a simple task, or an arduous, frustrating, and even dangerous affair. If you don't already have one, invest in a solid chef's knife, around 8–10 inches long, and sharpen it regularly. It will serve you well for a decade or more. In addition to a steel chef's knife, I also appreciate having a ceramic knife in the kitchen; it stays perfectly sharp so much longer, and is excellent for softer produce like tomatoes and onions.

I can't remember when or where I got my wooden soup spoon; all I know is, it's special to me…if only because it's made so, so many soups! (A wooden spoon is best because it won't scratch your pan.) Get a big spoon you love and grow old with it. If you're anything like me, this is the kind of tool that can be equal parts sentimentality and function.

Last, for some recipes, you'll need the ability to blend ingredients. In what seems to be a touchy subject among chefs, for whatever reason, there are two ways to blend soups—with an immersion blender (a stick-like device that you submerge directly into the soup pot) or a countertop blender. Personally, I vastly prefer a traditional blender to an immersion device, as I feel it produces a much smoother soup, and more quickly, too. Having said that, feel free to use an immersion blender to make any of the puréed recipes in this book, if it's more your style.

SUPERFOOD ESSENTIALS

There is no such thing as a perfect food—not even among superfoods. No single superfood is a 100 percent cure-all or has the power to give you full immunity from disease. But what superfoods *can* do is enhance any dish with highly dense forms of nutrition. Eating them thereby creates a healthy inner ecosystem that, in turn, leads to a stronger and better-balanced body. In short, the regular practice of consuming superfoods helps shape your best biological self.

Which brings us to the idea of The Superfood Seven: the families of superfoods that are the most readily available, are the most thoroughly studied and prized, and offer the best flavors and nutrition for soups. There are a thrilling number of wonderful superfoods in the world, but alas, some are still rather difficult to obtain, while others suffer from too much nutritional loss during cooking (more on that later). As a result, this list focuses on the best superfoods *for soups*, while keeping your health, wallet, and kitchen real estate in mind, too! The Superfood Seven are incredible resources to have in your healthy pantry.

THE SUPERFOOD SEVEN

Medicinal mushrooms
Sea vegetables
Green vegetables
Super berries
Super roots
Super seeds
Super grains

In high school, I spent a year up in northern Idaho. It was there that wayward students would occasionally sneak off campus, into the neighboring fields, to pick mushrooms (which, I'll just say, were not the culinary variety) off of cow dung. Mushrooms have a confusing rap, as they are often associated with poison (a few are), hallucinogens (so the cow-dung kids confirmed), or they've simply been deemed bad for you (a myth rooted in Western folklore, where some ancient English texts suggest that mushrooms are born of witches and can strangle whoever eats them). But these mycophobic cautions and tall tales quickly fade

when you compare them to the genuinely miraculous benefits of certain varieties of fungi—a class called medicinal mushrooms. These special strains excel in offering powerful immune support to prevent and fight a broad spectrum of diseases, thanks to a unique array of phytochemicals. In fact, even common culinary mushrooms are quite healthy in and of themselves, providing a good source of many micronutrients like B vitamins, iron, and vitamin C. And their meat-like flavor isn't just a figment of your imagination: mushrooms are considerably high in protein for their weight—a complete protein, in fact, with all of the essential amino acids.

The term *medicinal mushrooms* simply refers to the superfood version of "regular" mushrooms—they're special varieties of the same family, just as kale, compared to iceberg lettuce, is considered a superfood. Shiitake mushrooms, for example, enhance the immune system about 100 times more than white button mushrooms. So, while all mushrooms are beneficial, medicinal mushrooms go the extra mile, nutritionally speaking, and are well worth seeking out.

Benefits & Varieties I do not say this lightly: medicinal mushrooms earn their name as some of the most powerful, remedial superfoods you can possibly get your hands on. It is a difficult task to even attempt to sum up their ever-expanding repertoire of beneficial attributes (and contain my own enthusiasm) for them here. Medicinal mushrooms are filled with fascinating compounds, many of which are still being explored. For the sake of simplicity, you will find just five kinds of medicinal mushrooms in the recipes in this book, only two of which (shiitake and maitake) are available fresh or dried. The other three are sold in powdered form and have very little flavor, a quality which makes them especially easy to incorporate into recipes. In any case, I highly encourage you to soak up as much knowledge as you can about these outstanding foods, and choose the mushrooms that best meet your personal health goals.

Shiitake

Although shiitakes are the second most popular culinary mushroom in the world (after ubiquitous white button mushrooms), they confer an impressive array of medicinal benefits, while offering immensely pleasurable flavor. Shiitake mushrooms are used in traditional Chinese medicine to treat high cholesterol as well as colds and flu. Additionally, in past decades, studies have shown that LEM (lentinula edodes mycelia), a unique antioxidant element found in these special fungi, may inhibit tumor growth. This incredible discovery has inspired the development of a mushroom-derived anticancer drug that has been approved in Japan and is currently being used there to improve immune function. Because of its ability to stimulate antibodies, LEM is also considered helpful in cases of hepatitis, HIV, tooth decay, liver disease, and bacteria-related ailments. And, since the shiitake mushroom is so meaty and desirably rich in savory umami flavor, it is the most versatile and easy to use of the medicinal mushrooms. For all these reasons,

consider shiitake an excellent ingredient to add to soups and stews of all varieties.

Reishi

Some Eastern herbalists tout reishi mushrooms as "the king of herbal medicine"—and even rank them above ginseng, one of the most important and coveted components of traditional Chinese medicine. From a scientific standpoint, reishi mushrooms contain an array of important antioxidants and microelements, such as beta

THE IMPORTANCE OF UMAMI

Most of us are familiar with the four taste sensations in food: sweet, salty, bitter, and sour. But many years ago, science confirmed the presence of a fifth sense, called *umami*, loosely described as "savory" or "meaty." Technically speaking, this crave-worthy flavor is due to the presence of a common amino acid known as glutamine. While glutamine is most often present in high-protein foods like meat, it's also naturally concentrated in some plant-based foods like miso, seaweed, mushrooms, and even some fruits like tomatoes. Adding these umami-rich ingredients to your dishes can help create an exceptionally well-rounded flavor that has a lot of depth, transforming your recipes into something that just feels instinctually balanced and undeniably delicious.

glucans, ling zhi-8 protein, and ganodermic acids. If the names of these elements don't excite you, perhaps their benefits will: modern herbalists use reishi in a vast and impressive array of remedies that help combat chronic fatigue syndrome, diabetes, and high cholesterol, while assisting liver detoxification and promoting anti-allergic activity that ranges from hay fever to asthma. Some reishi-based remedies are even used cosmetically to protect and beautify the skin—and because of the mushroom's adaptogenic qualities, it's also an ideal superfood to use for stress-related symptoms, promoting overall adrenal balance. Although not classified as a culinary mushroom (it has a rather bitter flavor), reishi is considered a tonic and often used for teas. Since it is called for in such small quantities in soups, reishi's less-than-delicious taste can easily be masked with other vegetables and herbs.

Cordyceps

When you think of cordyceps (a genus of fungi that includes hundreds of species), think energy and vitality. Cordyceps are a favorite among athletes as a pre- and post-workout recovery tool that can effectively boost stamina and performance, thanks to their ability to enhance oxygen intake. And speaking of stamina and performance, cordyceps have also long been used in China to enhance or restore sexual function (in both men and women). In other clinical studies, they have been shown to lower bad cholesterol and increase good cholesterol. Even more health benefits of cordyceps include a salutary effect on lung and respiratory health, including bronchitis and asthma; and they are also considered a helpful tool in cases of diabetes and hepatitis B, and even liver and kidney disorders. Fatigue-fighting cordyceps have a lightly bitter taste (although less so than reishi), and can easily be incorporated into almost any kind of soup.

USING SWEETENERS IN SOUPS

Sugar is perhaps the world's most controversial ingredient (and understandably so). But, truly, not all sugars are created equal! Better-choice sweeteners, such as low-glycemic coconut sugar and mineral-inclusive natural maple syrup, work beautifully in all types of recipes. And, and believe it or not, they're sometimes needed to balance flavor in savory recipes, too. You won't use these sweeteners very often in the recipes in this book—and even when you do, you won't need to add very much (in fact, per-serving quantities use absolutely tiny amounts). Just keep in mind that the occasional touch of a smart sweetener, used with an abundance of other nutrient-dense foods, is nothing to fear.

Chaga

Because of its anti-inflammatory, antiviral, anti-fungal, and antitumor properties, the chaga mushroom's reputation continues to grow and make waves in medical communities all around the world. Chaga offers one of the highest supplies of a powerful antioxidant known as superoxide dismutase (SOD), vitamin D, important and unique minerals like zinc and germanium, and beta glucans, along with an enormous range of healing properties, including lowering blood pressure, decreasing blood sugar levels, and promoting healing for chronic stomach disorders. Yet it's chaga's anticancer activity, which ranges from cellular regeneration after chemotherapy to delaying some kinds of tumor growth, that is perhaps most revered. Indeed, chaga shows promise in helping prevent and heal a wide range of cancers, in particular melanoma, liver, bone, and stomach cancer. A must-have in any superfood collection, chaga has a mildly bitter taste that goes unnoticed, for the most part, in soups and stews.

How to Use Medicinal Mushrooms Thanks to their earthy, meaty flavor, fresh mushrooms can be enjoyed in all kinds of savory recipes, from sustaining broths to hearty chilis. Shiitakes have a more pronounced flavor presence than other medicinal mushrooms, as they are used whole, more often than not. Mushroom powders (reishi, cordyceps, and chaga) can be used in virtually any recipe with little influence on taste.

Important note: From a flavor standpoint, any of the mushroom powders called for in this book are interchangeable in a 1:1 ratio. For example, if you're really in need of chaga's health benefits, but the recipe calls for reishi, just swap them! You get the idea.

Honorable Mention: Maitake Mushrooms

Maitake is perhaps best known as a wild culinary mushroom (though it is often cultivated nowadays) and highly valued for its meaty flavor. When it is in season, you can find maitake at farmers markets and some grocery stores, for a couple of months, before they are gobbled up by excited chefs and in-the-know home cooks. Yet maitake is also a medicinal mushroom, traditionally used in Japanese medicine to boost the immune system and bolster vitality. After decades of modern research, maitake is now also touted as an effective tool to control diabetes, lower cholesterol, stabilize blood pressure, balance weight, and aid in the body's response against autoimmune diseases. While it is sold in powdered form, it is such a delicious mushroom that when I can find it, I can't help but use it fresh. As it is quite seasonal, just make a note-to-self to grab it in the market when you see it. It is rarely used in the recipes in this book, and may always be substituted for with another fresh mushroom variety.

SEA VEGETABLES

"If all foods could be made even moderately healthier...even functional, by the addition of specific seaweeds, [we could have] an effective long-term intervention strategy for [heart disease]." This was the concluding statement of scientists from the University of Southern Denmark in their 2015 paper published in *Phycologia,* after studying the health effects of no less than 35 different types of edible seaweed. Historically, seaweeds, otherwise known as sea vegetables and seagreens, have enjoyed a long use in just about every coastline community around the world, but are rarely used outside of "cultural" recipes in North America. Sea vegetables are nothing short of superfood soup heroes, valuable as both a food and a medicine. Use them every chance you can.

Benefits & Varieties Many people generalize seaweeds, lumping them together because they often look alike in their dried form. Yet seaweeds are as different in flavor and function as asparagus is from arugula. Gold star examples of nutrient density at work, seaweeds are extremely low in calories yet chock full of benefits: balanced macronutrients, amino acids, fiber, a favorable omega-3/omega-6 ratio, vitamins, antioxidants, and, most abundantly, minerals. Major players like alkaline-forming calcium, iron, magnesium, and sodium (electrolytes) abound in seaweeds, in addition to a bounty of important and rare trace minerals like metabolism-aiding molybdenum. Sea vegetables infuse nutrition into almost anything they are put into,

make foods like beans and legumes more digestible, lower the need for table salt (minerals taste salty), and offer a rich, savory umami flavor. In addition, the nutritional qualities of seagreens make them eminently helpful in the areas of bone and joint strength, immunity, cancer prevention and healing, skin health, detoxification, and balancing metabolism.

Kombu
Kombu, a brown seaweed, is sold as a culinary ingredient in thick dried slices and has been a core component of soup in East Asia for millennia. Brown seaweeds contain many antioxidants, and obtain their distinctive pigment from a rare compound known as fucoxanthin. Excitingly, preliminary studies have shown excellent results in fucoxanthin's ability to fight stomach problems, from infections to cancer, as effectively as antibiotics. Kombu is also a helpful metabolism booster, and it is often sold as a dietary supplement for this purpose.

Kelp
Another brown seaweed, kelp is one of the most traditional seaweed varieties used in soup. While it contains around 30 minerals, kelp is most revered for its impressive iodine content, and is thus extremely useful for supporting thyroid health. Kelp has quite a potent salty flavor, so it's easiest to use it in its powdered form (or in "kelp granules," as it is sometimes marketed) to control its strong flavor.

Dulse

Considered a red seaweed, dulse is grown in very deep waters, and is often sold in dried strips, flakes, or powder. Because of their texture and robust flavor, I find that flakes are the most efficient form of dulse to use in soups. (They are one of the most utilized superfoods in this book.) This seaweed offers strong antiviral benefits and is an excellent supply of trace minerals such as potassium, sodium, magnesium, calcium, zinc, chromium, and more.

Nori

Yes, nori is the beloved seaweed used to wrap and roll sushi. Despite its dark color, which appears greenish-black when pressed into sheets, nori is technically considered a red seaweed. It offers high levels of amino acids (protein) for its weight and size, and contains minerals similar to those in dulse. As a wonderful means of imparting a meaty flavor into recipes, you can use the same kind of dried nori sheets that you buy for sushi in soups.

Wakame

Although it appears green, wakame is considered a brown seaweed. It is commonplace in Asian cultures, where it is given to expecting and new mothers, thanks to its high levels of calcium and iodine. Wakame has a strong, slightly sweet seaweed flavor, and it is packaged and sold in a dry form. Be aware that wakame flakes expand substantially after just a few minutes of soaking

STORING SEAWEEDS

A huge advantage of seaweeds is that, unlike fresh (land) vegetables, seaweeds are sold dried, and can last for years without spoilage or loss of flavor or nutrition. I can attest to that: two years ago, I overzealously bought a pound of kelp powder, and while I'm still making my way through this enormous supply, it's as good as the day I bought it. Simply store dried seaweed in a sealed container to protect it from moisture, and keep it out of direct sunlight.

in a soup. I recommend crumbling them slightly before mixing them into the pot to yield more manageable pieces once they are hydrated.

How to Use Sea Vegetables Heavier seaweeds, such as kombu and kelp, are best added to savory soups toward the beginning of the cooking process, so their flavors have a chance to mellow and infuse with the soup. Lighter seaweeds, like nori and dulse, can be added at virtually any time during cooking, or even just at the end, as a garnish. Although seaweeds are surprisingly versatile and can be used in almost any kind of soup recipe, I find that their flavors work particularly well in creamy chowders and hearty stews, as well as in bean and grain (or noodle) soups.

GREEN VEGETABLES

The cardinal rule of healthy eating is "if it's green and edible, it's probably good for you"—no breaking news there! Flavorful green vegetables are the original superfoods—the healthiest of the healthy. And yet, despite knowing their virtues, many of us are still looking for better ways to incorporate more of them into our diet, hence the popularity of the ubiquitous (and wonderful) green smoothie. Believe it or not, soups are a dynamic part of the answer—the perfect venue for a casual addition of vibrant greens that help lighten heavy flavors and balance nutrition. Plus, whether they're blended or tossed in at the last minute, it's exciting to see how quickly salad-size handfuls of greens seem to shrink down in soups, allowing you to easily enjoy the equivalent of a huge serving in a hearty—yet manageable—mouthwatering form.

Benefits & Varieties Filled with detoxifying, immune-boosting, anti-inflammatory properties, green vegetables abound in nutrients like vitamins A, C, E, and K; folic acid; calcium; iron; manganese; protein; fiber…you'll run out of breath before you can finish naming all the benefits! Rich in flavonoids, from deeply alkaline chlorophyll to antitumor carotene, these potent disease fighters are a gold mine of antioxidant activity, too. Greens are ubiquitously the most highly regarded food among dietitians, nutrition scientists, doctors, and health experts, regardless of individual doctrine. There's simply no denying the power of green.

Happily, there are so many types of green vegetables from which to choose! Some of the best veggies for soups include leafy greens like **kale, spinach, arugula, Swiss chard,** and **watercress.** On the more robust side are cruciferous greens such as **cabbage, Brussels sprouts,** and **broccoli** (all well-known anticancer foods). Amplifying the medicinal qualities even further are fresh herbs like **parsley, rosemary, thyme,** and **cilantro,** whose potent flavor is nature's indicator of medicinal and protective phytonutrients at work. (Ever notice how insects and garden pests usually leave herbs alone? That's phytochemicals in action, protecting the plant from damage—and they can do the same for you, too.) And last, but most certainly not least, there are sprouts and grasses—**sunflower sprouts** and **wheatgrass,** for example—which, in their "baby" form, contain elevated levels of micronutrients, especially when compared to mature plants.

How to Use Green Vegetables With the exception of a couple of the protective qualities in fresh herbs and cruciferous vegetables, most of the major nutrients in green vegetables are rather sensitive to heat degradation, thus they are best used in recipes that require minimal to no cooking at all. To preserve their nutrients, add leafy greens at the end of cooking; blend grasses into sauces, like pesto (before adding it to a soup); chop herbs and sprouts finely and use them as a refreshing topping; or blend your green variety of choice into a cold soup. This is not to say these foods will develop a poor taste with extended cooking, but many of their superfood qualities will be lost.

Honorable Mention: Algae

Although it is not exactly a green vegetable, super-food forms of algae, like **spirulina** and **chlorella**, are without question among the very best superfoods you can eat. The nutrients are so concentrated in spirulina, for example, that to match the nutritional gains of consuming just 3 grams of this blue-green algae, you'd have to eat about 500 grams of fruits and vegetables. Energizing, detoxifying, immune-boosting . . . the list of superlative qualities that describe algae's healthful impact goes on and on.

While spirulina and chlorella have a multitude of culinary uses (in smoothies, dips, and dressings, for example), their use is, admittedly, limited in soup making: algae cannot be cooked/exposed to heat for very long without compromised nutritional benefits. So, to preserve those benefits, I suggest using algae in chilled green soups (or in chilled soups that are not green if you don't care what your soup looks like), or whisking algae into saucy toppings that go on top of hot soups. Since algae is one of my all-time favorite superfoods, I've snuck it into a few recipes in this book, but you won't find it in too many places due to its culinary limitations.

With the exception of a gazpacho, most people don't think of fruit when they think of soup. And while there are many berries that don't make the cut, surprisingly, there are a few varieties that not only can stand up to a savory warm recipe, but also truly shine. These superfoods serve a couple of purposes in the context of soup recipes: they add plenty of nutrition, of course, but they also add unique flavors—even sometimes a subtle sweetness that can replace refined sugar. Sweetening with superfoods? Now, that's a winning solution.

Benefits & Varieties Fruit is often called nature's candy, which always makes me laugh—if only our version of candy were even 1/100th as good for us! All fruits contain their own unique stores of vitamins and antioxidants. "Super fruits," such as berries, just take all those benefits and condense them into smaller, lower-calorie, and more highly saturated nutritional packages. Each of the berries used in this book is wildly different, but every one of them has something in common: longevity. Believe it or not, once you've made your initial super fruit investment (see the list that follows), you can relax and enjoy their long shelf life and benefits for months.

Camu Berries

Camu, a cranberry-like berry that is native to Amazonian floodplains and usually sold in powdered form in North America, is rarely a call-out ingredient on menus, due to its rather bitter flavor. It is extremely low in sugar (did I mention it's bitter?), but what camu lacks in deliciousness it makes up in one important nutrient: vitamin C. Research has shown that camu is the most concentrated natural source of this

anti-inflammatory vitamin of all foods, and it is so potent that even just a pinch of it can get you close to your daily requirements! You can't cook with camu, or its sensitive nutrition will be lost, but it is nevertheless an excellent "boost" ingredient that can be tucked into chilled soups and uncooked sauces.

Goji Berries

This may come as a surprise: dried goji berries are one of the very best superfoods for soup! Although they are a fruit—a little red berry that, when fresh, looks like a Roma tomato that has shrunk down to the size of a peanut—goji berries are only slightly sweet, with a nuanced flavor spectrum that includes notes of tomato, citrus, pepper, and smoke. A top-tier superfood by anyone's calculations, goji berries are a profoundly complete food, with high-grade protein, low-glycemic carbohydrates, antioxidant-rich fat, and more than 20 vitamins and minerals to boot. Research points to an impressive concentration of healing antioxidants in the tiny berry, with studies showing promise in its power to support eye, brain, and heart health, as well as improve memory (and help stave off Alzheimer's disease). Goji berries even help keep skin healthy from the inside out, through their powerful amounts of anti-aging and protective agents, like carotene.

On the flavor spectrum, since goji berries can swing from sweet to savory, they have a particular affinity for tomato-based soups and recipes that feature summer vegetables, fall squashes, and hearty beans. You'll mostly find goji berries in dried form.

Goldenberries

A veritable explosion of sweet and sour flavors, there's no hiding the exciting taste of a dried goldenberry; it demands to be celebrated with cohesive ingredients, or it will hit the override button and simply take over. Goldenberries are closely related to the tomatillo (that husk-covered green tomato thing you sometimes see at the market during warm weather) and are often called by many names (you may, in fact, already know them as cape gooseberries). An excellent source of vitamins A and C, goldenberries are famous for their anti-inflammatory properties, and they contain bioavailable quercetin—a flavonoid used to treat conditions such as atherosclerosis, high cholesterol, heart disease, asthma, and viral infections. Thanks to this restorative nutrition, goldenberries are also used to improve athletic performance and hasten recovery.

In their sun-dried form, goldenberries are available year-round (and are much less expensive than fresh goldenberries). They are at their best in summertime soups, which appreciate a little fruit, or in citrus-y chutneys to top a hearty stew.

Sea Buckthorn Berries

This incredible berry thrives in seaside locations, as its name suggests, where it grows on thorny branches that hold heavy clusters of berries at a time—quite an eye-catching sight with their standout orange hue. Sea buckthorn, which is mostly found as a shelf-stable juice in North America (see page 219 for sources), tastes citrus-y with a hint of honey—and although the juice is more sour than sweet, the flavor is balanced with a luxuriously smooth and ever so slightly creamy texture. While sea buckthorn contains many nutrients that are typical of other berries, such as vitamins A and C, it is unusual because of its fat content. In fact, sea buckthorn is one of the few fruits in the world that contains a balance of omega-3, omega-6, and omega-9 fats, as well as the exceptionally rare omega-7 fat—the newest "good" fat on the block, which is becoming well known for its positive effects on cholesterol levels, liver health, maintaining a healthy weight, and protecting against type 2 diabetes. Although sea buckthorn may be new to most of our kitchen pantries, it is already widely used in the beauty industry as a powerful anti-aging, glow-inducing topical ingredient in high-end lotions and skin treatments. With the same—if not greater—ability to beautify us from the inside out, sea buckthorn is without question a valuable soup ingredient. It is particularly delicious in delicate, creamy soups and in light, citrus-inflected fruit soups.

How to Use Super Berries Super berries like goji berries (which are practically ubiquitous in this book) and goldenberries—can waltz into virtually any soup that can use a little bit of sweetness. Other super berries, such as camu and sea buckthorn, should be used more selectively—that is, primarily in raw or lightly cooked soups—in order to preserve their considerable nutritional benefits.

Honorable Mention: Pomegranate

Pomegranates are such a miraculous superfood: they not only taste great (who can resist the sweet-sour juicy pop of fresh pomegranate seeds?) but offer powerful medicine as well, including high amounts of micronutrients such as potassium, vitamin K, vitamin C, and special compounds known as punicalagins (antioxidants) and punicic acid (a type of conjugated linoleic acid, aka a really "good" fat). Regular consumption of anti-inflammatory pomegranate is deemed helpful in lowering blood pressure, preventing and fighting many kinds of cancer cells (including breast and prostate), easing joint pain and arthritis, and improving memory. While pomegranate is most nutritionally useful uncooked and isn't the most go-to ingredient for stirring into a soup, the fresh seeds make a wonderful superfood topping for root-, tuber-, and squash-based soups (see page 126 to make Persimmon Holiday Soup and fall in love). Just sprinkle the seeds on top of your soup right before serving for a dynamic presentation, healthy boost, and delicious treat!

It makes sense that roots are so potent—they are like reverse antennae, reaching down into the nourishing soil and acting like magnets to pull all the moisture and nutrients out of the ground before transferring them upward, into the plant's foliage. While all edible roots and tubers (carrots, parsnips, turnips, radishes, and so many more!) are very healthy, some are downright medicinal and have enjoyed a long history of traditional use in curing a litany of ailments. These are super roots, such as turmeric, ginger, maca, and yacon—foods that take nutrition to the next level of amazingly good for you. It is equally gratifying to discover how easy it is to use these delicious, invigorating superfoods—and how ideal they are for making and flavoring soups.

Benefits & Varieties The nutritional blueprint of most plants follows a similar plan: there are more vitamins at the top of the plant (in the foliage), and more minerals down below (in the roots), with antioxidants mostly indifferent to location. But while many super roots are celebrated for their high levels of important minerals such as iron and the like, they are even better known for the extraordinary plant compounds, known as phytochemicals, which they also contain. These special compounds substantially elevate the value of super roots—like ginger and maca—not just because they are superb ingredients for alluring soups, but because they can genuinely help heal and protect our bodies as well.

Ginger
The unique flavor of ginger, with its spicy, sweet, and floral notes, makes it one of the most commonly used spices in the world. Yet ginger is more than just a pretty taste—one look at its therapeutic benefits makes it clear that it is, in fact, a bona fide superfood. Hooray for a superfood that most of us already use and love!

Throughout history, it has been purported that ginger has the power to soothe hundreds of ailments, and recent scientific studies have confirmed this ancient claim. Like other medicinal superfoods (such as fresh herbs or chaga mushrooms), the most significant healing factors in ginger are not found in the micronutrients it contains, such as vitamin A and calcium, but

WHAT'S THE DIFFERENCE BETWEEN A ROOT AND A TUBER?

Roots are directly connected to a plant and serve as a freeway for nutrients and moisture to travel from the earth up to the leaves. Examples of root vegetables include carrots, beets, and radishes. Tubers, on the other hand, are not directly connected to a plant. Instead, they are connected to a root system via an underground stem, and act like a storage system for extra nutrients and moisture. Commonly known tubers include potatoes, yams, and jicama.

rather in phytochemical compounds, namely metabolites. These compounds make ginger a powerful antioxidant, anti-inflammatory, anti-nausea, and anticancer agent. So, while ginger may be a relatively small root, it is mighty in both flavor and function. It is best used in its fresh form in soups, where its delicious and invigorating benefits can be enjoyed in unlimited ways.

Maca

Maca really is in a superfood class of its own. An amazing plant that thrives in areas of the Andean highlands of Peru, where few other plants are strong enough to grow, maca is revered as an adaptogen—a food that actually adapts and adjusts to the biological needs of your body, helping to balance stress levels, hormones, sex drive, and overall energy. On a personal note, when I was 20 years old, maca was one of the first superfoods I ever used, and I credit my recovery from the symptoms of chronic fatigue syndrome largely to this incredible root. Maca is most often sold as a powder in North America, and lends a malty, slightly sweet, somewhat earthy flavor to soups. I find it to be an especially harmonious ingredient in recipes that contain other roots as well.

Turmeric

Known for its intense, marigold-yellow color and spectrum of mellow-bitter-gingery-peppery-floral flavor, turmeric has long been used as a culinary spice as well as in Ayurvedic medicine. Turmeric's most important attribute is its concentration of curcumin, an antioxidant so potent in anti-inflammatory benefits, that it is sold as a natural form of ibuprofen. Curcumin is also what makes turmeric so promising as a cancer-fighting food, by helping the body destroy mutated cells. The use of turmeric in healing is widespread, and many consider it to be a fundamental superfood. You will find it in Eastern-inflected soups (if ginger is a component, it will often be accompanied by turmeric), and since the flavor of turmeric is so mild in small doses (½ teaspoon or less), you can sneak it into all kinds of soups for a powerfully healing boost. While it is becoming easier to find fresh turmeric in some stores (it's usually sold right next to ginger in the produce section), you can use turmeric powder just as effectively and beneficially in soups and also take advantage of the lower cost of the powder.

Yacon

Yacon, the tuber of a hardy perennial plant that grows in Peru, has long been treasured in South America for its medicinal uses, such as helping with diabetes. It is eaten and enjoyed as a whole root, dried into slices as a tasty snack, and concentrated into a syrup and used as a natural sweetener. But what makes yacon so special (over and above its high content of amino acids, potassium, calcium, phosphorus, and iron) is its concentration of inulin, a type of diabetic-friendly sugar and a prebiotic. Prebiotics are the indigestible dietary fibers that come from the foods we eat and directly help probiotics grow and function (probiotics promote the growth of healthy bacteria in the digestive tract and act as food for the types of good bacteria that our bodies need to be healthy). Chewy dried yacon slices taste like a smoky apple, and they are great as a soup topping—or, they can be boiled with other ingredients to release their impressive flavor into the soup. Yacon syrup is an excellent low-glycemic ingredient in soups that need extra sweetness, and it can even be drizzled on top of squash soups and chili as a final flavor burst.

How to Use Super Roots With the exception of yacon, each of the super roots used in the recipes in this book has quite a strong flavor on its own and is not the type of root that you can use as abundantly as, say, carrots. Rather, super roots are best used much as you might employ fresh herbs, to balance and support flavors—and they pair with grains, tubers, and higher-fat soups particularly well. As an ingredient, yacon is a little more flexible; it can be added to virtually any soup that needs a little sweetness.

There is nothing that will get you into "Health Foodies Anonymous" faster than a well-curated collection of culinary seeds on the shelves of your pantry (or if you're like me, your super seeds are displayed, braggingly in plain sight, in glass jars all along the kitchen counter). Embrace them, my friend, as this humble class of foods is one that you're going to want to reach for every day. They're the littlest superfoods with something very big and mighty to prove.

Benefits & Varieties When you think about it, seeds are pretty remarkable things—they're the just-add-water "eggs" of the plant-based world that contain all of the proteins, fats, starches, and micronutrients needed to grow an entire plant. And in terms of their nutritional benefits, seeds are like nuts on steroids (if steroids could make you more powerful but actually smaller, rather than larger, that is). While all seeds offer at least some protein and fiber, each of the best super seeds boasts its own nuances, both in taste and healthy activity.

Quinoa

It may act like a grain, but gluten-free quinoa is just a little seed, with a whole lot of robust, delicious potential (hence its enormous popularity). Quinoa does more than just taste good; it also offers 8 grams of complete protein per cooked cup, along with fiber and a broad range of minerals like magnesium and zinc. It's also a particularly good source of skin-healthy manganese, which is essential for collagen production, the protein found in the connective tissue responsible for healthy joints and supple skin.

Amaranth

As if quinoa's protein content wasn't already good enough, along comes amaranth to top it at 9 grams of complete protein per cooked cup, including all the essential amino acids. This ancient Aztec food offers a true wealth of micronutrients, like iron, potassium, zinc, copper, and vitamin B6. Amaranth is even smaller than quinoa, and when it's cooked in water, it creates a porridge-like thickness that is excellent for hearty soups.

Chia

This pinhead-sized seed epitomizes a superfood: it may be tiny in size, yet it positively bursts with nutrition. Chia is best known for its exceptional quantity of omega-3s (eight times the amount in salmon, ounce for ounce) and minerals like calcium (up to seven times more calcium than dairy milk). Just 2 tablespoons of chia also provides almost one quarter of your daily fiber requirements and serves up 4 grams of complete protein. The phytonutrients in chia are also impressive, including anti-inflammatory quercetin, as well as chlorogenic acid and caffeic acid—both known metabolism-boosting elements. Almost nonexistent in flavor, chia seeds can be added to pretty much any kind of food. They will be slightly crunchy when added as a topping, or will swell up and thicken soups without adding many calories when cooked or left to sit in liquid.

Hemp

Who would have thought that one of the world's greatest sources of protein could be contained in a humble little seed? As you may have already summarized in this section, seeds are one of nature's densest sources of protein, and hemp tops the list, supplying 5 grams of complete protein in just 1½ tablespoons! What's more, the protein in hemp is alkaline-forming and extremely easy to digest (it will never give you a weighed-down feeling after eating it), and better still, hemp is procured from a drought-resistant, highly eco-friendly crop (an environmental quality few protein sources can boast). Like chia, hemp is also an exceptional source of omega-3s, as well as GLA—a rare type of omega-6 that is considered extremely helpful in many inflammatory conditions of the skin, joints, and brain. Hemp is also generous with its minerals, offering good supplies of iron, magnesium, potassium, and zinc. Soft and chewy, hemp's sunflower seed-like flavor is easy to fall in love with.

How to Use Super Seeds Quinoa and amaranth must be cooked before you can eat them, so the easiest way to prepare these seeds is to simply toss them in with your soup ingredients when you add the broth, and cook on your merry way until they're tender (after about 15–20 minutes). Although super seeds can take the place of pasta (as far as starchy texture goes), they're especially great for the absent-minded chef who is prone to forget about timing: super seeds, unlike pasta, do not get mushy if they're overcooked. As far as culinary applications go, the sky's the limit for hemp and chia seeds. These little powerhouses add texture to recipes without challenging their overall flavor and add a subtle creaminess when they're blended in. If you haven't used super seeds before, start simple—just sprinkle hemp or chia seeds on top of soups, as a natural garnish.

Honorable Mention: Cacao

Believe it or not, cacao is actually a large seed (even though it is confusingly called a cacao "bean"). And even more surprisingly, this raw form of

SOURCING SUPERFOODS

As the well-deserved fame of superfoods continues to grow, these incredible ingredients are becoming more readily available worldwide, in all types of stores. Most natural food stores carry the superfoods listed below, and increasingly, conventional markets may offer some as well. If you are having trouble finding superfoods locally, you can easily order them online—I've listed my favorite sites and sources in the Ingredient Resources Guide on page 219.

chocolate can be used as a wonderful soup ingredient from time to time. Cacao, or *real* chocolate, as I like to call it, is a mega source of minerals, like magnesium and iron, and supplies an abundance of antioxidants that protect the heart, skin, and brain—all good reasons for cacao's place on so many "best of" superfood lists!

Long before it was used as an ingredient in the chocolate bars we all know and love, cacao was celebrated as an energy food in ancient Central American cultures, where it was ground, mixed with hot water and spices, and enjoyed, unsweetened, as a drink. This concoction may have been considered a beverage, but I think it comes closer to being a soup! Semantics aside, cacao powder is a really lovely flavoring element that can be added in small quantities to the occasional soup or stew, particularly those that have a tomato base, are bean-centric, or offer a Mexican flair such as in chilis. However you use it, cacao certainly makes for a fun "secret ingredient."

Happily, grains are among the least expensive superfood ingredients and add a toothsome, hearty base to a great many soups. They are one of the most ancient cultivated foods, and there are thousands of nuanced varieties of grains in the world, although very few are seen in mainstream Western markets today. Most of the grains we use are hybridized strains, created through natural grafting (not GMO practices), in the hope of producing a crop that is more pest-resistant, higher in yield, and well suited to modern tastes. In other words, the wheat used today in whole-wheat flour is not the same wheat variety that the Egyptians so carefully cultivated. So, it's understandable why grains with such an ancient pedigree are so valuable. They simply are closest to the way nature intended them to be, before we crossbred and contaminated their natural makeup.

Ancient varieties of grain have a sturdier composition than their modern counterparts, often boasting much higher levels of the important nutrients that seem so hard to come by in the standard North American diet. In other words, these are the super grains, the best of their class, with the highest levels of nutrients. As they've become more popular, more varieties of super grains are showing up in the marketplace. For the sake of simplicity, I've used just a few of them in the recipes in this book, but I encourage you to get to know them all and reap the considerable rewards of adding them to your diet. They are a fantastic addition to soups.

Benefits & Varieties When most of us think of protein, grains aren't exactly the first things to come to mind, but they should be! Whole grains and, in particular, ancient grains are truly excellent sources of protein (for example, the sandwich bread we have at my house is made with sprouted whole grains, and offers 6 grams of protein per slice!). Ancient grains also contain excellent levels of dietary fiber, B vitamins, folate (spelt and farro, both considered "heirloom wheat," contain 50 percent more folate than modern wheat, for example), as well as minerals like selenium, potassium, phosphorus, and calcium. They are often rich in antioxidants and have long been recognized as a heart-healthy food.

Farro

One of the most popular ancient super grains is farro, a primitive form of wheat, widely celebrated for its boldly chewy, pleasantly nutty qualities. The use of farro dates back to ancient Egypt—it has even been found in the tombs of pharaohs (a phonetic irony). Farro actually refers to three types of grain (just as there are several varieties of rice): einkorn, which is the smallest type of farro; emmer, which is medium-sized; and spelt, the largest type, often simply called farro. If you find this classification confusing, you are not alone: labeling can be a bit of an issue! These days, farro/spelt is mostly sold as a semi-pearled variety, which dramatically cuts down cooking time, since it can be added, without an overnight soak, to soups at the last minute.

Sorghum (aka Milo)

This round gluten-free grain looks similar to pearled couscous. It offers a slightly sweet, neutral flavor and has been used as an ingredient in cooking since 8000 BC! Many environmentalists today are eyeing sorghum, which is sometimes referred to as "the camel of crops," and as a "crop of the future," because it is so hardy and requires very little water (about a third of what corn needs) to grow. Nutritionally, sorghum is on par with quinoa, offering high protein as well as anti-inflammatory and antioxidant nutrients. Sorghum is a great swap for all kinds of grains, pasta, corn, and rice, and it can even be popped into popcorn.

Freekeh

Freekeh is the name for hard wheat (usually durum) that's harvested when the plant is still young and green, and then toasted and cracked. Freekeh's chewy, barley-like texture is easy to fall in love with, and its benefits are many. Because freekeh is harvested young, it contains higher levels of easily digestible protein and micronutrients than mature wheat. But of freekeh's many healthful traits, perhaps the best known is its incredible fiber content—twice the amount of quinoa, and three times the amount of brown rice! This fiber, along with freekeh's unique form of resistant starch (a carbohydrate that passes through the digestive tract unchanged), means that freekeh is especially helpful in promoting healthy digestion, balancing blood sugar levels, and offering a long-lasting sense of fullness—a boon for anyone trying to manage a healthy weight.

How to Use Super Grains The great thing about super grains is that you can use them in recipes, just like regular grains—so swap away as you please! And although some recipes call for precooked grains (such as sorghum, which takes about an hour of cooking to become tender), most super grains can be added uncooked to recipes. Just allow them to simmer, along with the rest of the ingredients, and they'll add great flavor to the broth as they cook away. Alternatively, to make a heartier meal, you can cook a batch of super grains ahead of time, as a side dish, and serve it next to the soup.

Honorable Mention: Buckwheat

Despite its namesake, buckwheat is not related to wheat. It is actually a seed, even though it is most commonly classified as a cereal grain. Buckwheat is exceptionally easy to digest, and with almost 6 grams of protein and high levels of fiber and iron per serving, it's understandable why buckwheat maintains such a devoted following in the health scene. Although it's not widely used in soups (buckwheat is a little more starchy than, say, sorghum), it's a great ingredient to use in porridge, in the form of (hulled) buckwheat groats. You can also use buckwheat noodles made from buckwheat flour, which impart a slightly nutty flavor that's particularly pleasurable in Asian-influenced soups.

ADDITIONAL SUPERFOODS

With our ever-growing infatuation with longevity, youth, healing, and increased energy, countless foods, old and new, are being touted as the next big thing. And just because they're not included in the pages here, doesn't mean you shouldn't try them. In fact, I hope this book serves as a launching pad for you to explore and experience the limitless boundaries of a healthy, superfood-inclusive lifestyle. If you're itching to expand your superfood knowledge beyond the scope of the aforementioned ingredients, here are some additional soup-friendly superfoods and medicinal herbs to try:

* Aloe vera
* Ashwagandha
* Astralagus
* Burdock root
* Coffee berry
* Flaxseeds
* He shou wu
* Holy Basil (tulsi)
* Medicinal mushrooms (additional varieties such as lion's mane and turkey tail)
* Moringa
* Mucuna pruriens
* Rhodiola
* Sacha inchi seeds
* Seaweeds (additional varieties such as arame and sea palm)
* Rice bran (tocos)

HOW COOKING AFFECTS SUPERFOOD NUTRITION

In some ways, nutrition isn't as simple as it once was—it seems that the more we learn, the more complicated the nuances of micronutrients and their effects on the body become to interpret! For this reason, many of us are understandably concerned about how certain nutrients interact with heat during cooking. I get it: if you're spending quite a bit of money on some of these spectacular superfoods, it's important to get the nutrition you paid for! But before we categorize which superfoods are okay to cook, the bigger question to answer is what happens to *nutrients* when they are cooked.

Macronutrients (Carbohydrates, Protein, Fat, Fiber). The numerical content of all macronutrients stays the same, regardless of method preparation, whether it involves cooking or not. Note that some fats oxidize more quickly than others: cooking a superfood that contains high quantities of omega fats, like chia, for example, is fine, as long as the cooking temperature is not too high. Experts disagree on the exact temperature, but the general wisdom is that 400°F or less is best for ingredients with high omega content.

Vitamins. This class of micronutrients is somewhat more sensitive compared to, say, minerals. Some fat-soluble vitamins, like vitamin A, are relatively heat-stable and can withstand boiling water. However, other vitamins, like water-soluble vitamin C, are very sensitive to heat (and light and air, for that matter) and begin to degrade quickly when exposed. Note that the level at which these nutrients become compromised will also depend upon the temperature and method of cooking: simply placing a vitamin C–rich food in a skillet for 2 minutes will not necessarily "kill" all of the vitamin C immediately—only a percentage will be lost, while more will be lost during long periods of cooking, as is typical with slowly simmered soups. The loss of the B vitamin family in cooking also varies, but most of them will generally withstand cooking, with a few exceptions like riboflavin, folate, and pantothenic acid.

Minerals. Minerals are the easiest micronutrient group to understand in the realm of nutrient to cooking relationships (even though minerals are more difficult to obtain outside of very nutrient-dense foods, such as superfoods). They are not affected at all by heat in cooking... or any other method of preparation, for that matter.

Antioxidants. Here is where nutrition gets complex: some antioxidants, such as polyphenols, break down quickly when they are exposed to temperatures above 400°F. Others, like lycopene, actually have *increased* levels of absorption when they are heated, which explains why cooked tomatoes are widely thought to be "healthier" than raw tomatoes. By and large, unless you're specifically after one type of antioxidant, the phrase "you win some, you lose some" pretty much sums up the effect of cooking on antioxidants.

BLACK SUPERFOODS

If you're looking for the "new black" in nutrition, it's, well, black. Most natural foods come in all kinds of varieties and heirloom types, although only a fraction of them have been introduced to the consumer market. Thankfully, that's beginning to change with the whole foods movement, which celebrates biocentric diversity within different crops, and seeks to enhance options to put on our dinner plates. Among these varied crops, you can sometimes find black strains that taste the same as their non-black counterparts but offer unique benefits. These foods include black ("forbidden") rice, black lentils, black quinoa, black beans, and black sesame seeds, as well as black carrots and radishes. When you see this color in nature, what you're really seeing is a huge superfood upgrade: a large presence of anthocyanin antioxidants, a type of flavonoid or plant pigment. Anthocyanins are most often thought of as the purple-blue antioxidant, which is responsible for making blueberries blue and grapes purple. When there is an extremely high concentration of anthocyanins in a bean or a seed or a vegetable, a fruit, or a grain, it appears to be black (and also explains why water turns slightly purple after you've soaked black rice in it). Anthocyanins are among the most studied cancer-fighting antioxidants of our time, and they have also been linked to a long list of benefits, including heart and skin health, as well as athletic stamina. You probably won't notice much of a flavor difference whether the grains or veggies you eat are black; nevertheless, black foods are often nature's way of announcing "Now with more!"

Understanding how heat affects different nutritional components is key to determining whether to cook a superfood or use it raw (in order to reap its full nutritional potential). For example, camu powder is most celebrated for its massive vitamin C content, meaning it is best used in unheated applications. Cacao offers an impressive mineral content, as well as high polyphenols, so although high heat can diminish some of its antioxidant potential, it still offers many benefits, whether cooked or raw. Maca is primarily rich in minerals, so it can stand up to just about any cooking method, although it tastes best in hot soups.

The bottom line is that there's really no black-or-white "best" method (cooked versus raw) for preparing food, as a whole, to obtain optimum nutrition; each ingredient must be taken into account. But it's not difficult to maximize your results (and certainly nothing to stress over). To get the most benefits—nutrition, digestibility, and more—from the superfoods used in this book, simply use the following cheat sheet for all your future healthy cooking endeavors.

COOKING WITH SUPERFOODS CHEAT SHEET

SUPERFOOD	TYPE	TECHNIQUE
Amaranth	Super grain	Must be cooked, but may be used in hot or cold soups.
Buckwheat	Super grain	Must be cooked, but may be used in hot or cold soups.
Camu	Super berry	Use in cold soups or as a garnish (do not cook).
Chaga	Medicinal mushroom	Use in hot or cold soups.
Chia	Super seed	Use in hot or cold soups, or as a garnish. Do not heat over 400°F.
Cordyceps	Medicinal mushroom	Use in hot or cold soups.
Cruciferous greens	Green vegetable	Best used in hot soups, or as a raw garnish.
Dulse	Sea vegetable	Use in hot or cold soups, or as a garnish.
Farro	Super grain	Must be cooked, but may be used in hot or cold soups.
Freekeh	Super grain	Must be cooked, but may be used in hot or cold soups.
Ginger	Super root	Use in hot or cold soups.
Goji berries	Super berry	Use in hot or cold soups, or as a garnish.
Goldenberries	Super berry	Best used in cold soups, or as a garnish.
Hemp seeds	Super seed	Use in hot or cold soups, or as a garnish.

SUPERFOOD	TYPE	TECHNIQUE
Herbs	Green vegetable	Okay to use in hot soups, but more nutritious when added near the end of cooking. Good used in cold soups or as a garnish.
Leafy greens	Green vegetable	Okay to use in hot soups, but add at the very end of cooking. Good used in cold soups, or as a garnish.
Maca powder	Super root	Best in hot soups, but may be used in cold soups.
Nori	Sea vegetable	Use in hot or cold soups, or as a garnish.
Pomegranate seeds	Super fruit	Use in cold soups, or as a garnish.
Reishi	Medicinal mushroom	Use in hot or cold soups.
Sea buckthorn	Super berry	Use in cold soups, or as a garnish.
Shiitake	Medicinal mushroom	Use in hot or cold soups.
Sorghum	Super grain	Must be cooked, but may be used in hot or cold soups.
Spirulina (or chlorella)	Algae	Use in cold soups, or as a garnish (do not cook).
Sprouts	Green vegetable	Use as a garnish.
Turmeric	Super root	Use in hot or cold soups.
Wheatgrass powder	Green vegetable	Use in cold soups, or as a garnish (do not cook).
Yacon	Super root	Use in hot or cold soups.

THE TRUE COST OF INGREDIENTS

The first wealth is health.
—Ralph Waldo Emerson

Let's put the obvious flavor and proven health advantages of homemade soup aside for a moment. Is it *easier* to open a can of soup and call it dinner? Absolutely. But is it less expensive? Well, that depends on the price you're willing to pay. Allow me to explain.

Many people look at the back of a product label and glance over the nutrition facts. While this is a good start for conscious consumption, it's a little akin to looking at a disease without questioning what caused it. The real story of a recipe lies in the ingredients, and in the case of some canned soups, these ingredients may shock you: high fructose corn syrup. Monopotassium phosphate. Partially hydrogenated soybean oil. "Flavoring." The common inclusion of these types of additives is astounding. Even the label on a simple-sounding soup, such as tomato, might contain a long list of preservatives, emulsifiers, artificial colorings, and more—which can lead to an equally long list of health risks, ranging from allergic reactions to mineral imbalances and even carcinogenic effects. *That's* quite a high cost.

Of course, there are many alternative canned brands these days that offer a cleaner list of ingredients. But you'll be happy to discover that not only is making your own superfood soups a wonderful investment in your health, it's also a surprisingly inexpensive practice (even less expensive than making your own smoothies!). And while there might be an initial outlay to set up shop—that is, buying a small curation of superfood ingredients (unless, of course, you are already well stocked)—do not fear. Many of the more costly ingredients used in *Superfood Soups* are used over and over again—and in very small quantities—so they'll last for a long time. In other words, when you look at the actual per-serving cost of superfood soups, it is surprisingly low.

At just a little over $2 per serving—less than the cost of a Caffe Latte at Starbucks or a so-called energy bar at the supermarket—the per-cup price of a homemade superfood soup is not only competitive with the cost of many organic canned soups, it may also cost about half the price of some fresh-made, packaged soups. Plus, you can feel even better, knowing that your money is going toward food that is dramatically more abundant in nourishment, as opposed to a packaged soup that contains lots of filler ingredients. When you buy superfoods, you are not just purchasing calories; you're getting the healthiest, most nutrient-dense foods money can buy. And beyond your happy taste buds, your body *always* knows the difference.

PER-SERVING* COST OF ROASTED CAULIFLOWER CHOWDER (PAGE 163):

* 1 medium head cauliflower	$3.00
* 3 tablespoons coconut oil	$0.64
* Sea salt and ground black pepper	n/a
* 1 yellow onion	$0.65
* 4 stalks celery	$1.00
* 3 cloves garlic	$0.16
* 1 tablespoon fresh thyme leaves	$0.40
* 2 bay leaves	$0.18
* 1 pound Yukon gold potatoes	$0.99
* ⅛ teaspoon cayenne pepper	$0.02
* 5 cups Seaweed Broth (page 64)	$1.20
* 2 tablespoons tahini	$0.65

* 1 tablespoon fresh lemon juice	$0.25
* ¼ cup minced fresh chives	$1.99
* 1 tablespoon dulse flakes	$0.19
* ¼ cup toasted pine nuts	$2.24

Cost per serving (serving = 1⅓ cups): **$2.26**
Total recipe cost: **$13.56**

*Recipe makes six 1⅓-cup servings. Costs are approximations based on full retail price, using 100% organic, local, seasonal produce wherever possible. The final cost may vary slightly.

STORING SOUP

It's a smart move to make soup ahead of time (I often double my own soup recipes so that I can reap the rewards many times over). And soup is just the kind of recipe you can make on a weekend and enjoy throughout the week for easy meals. This is perhaps one of soup's best advantages: you can make it at your leisure and save it for later—a delicious gift that keeps on giving!

When storing fresh soups, it's helpful to use the same principles as a professional kitchen. In other words, safety should come first. When working with hot soup, avoid transferring it directly from the stove to the refrigerator. This can, potentially, sharply raise the temperature of the air in the refrigerator, putting other foods at risk of spoilage. Instead, let the soup cool to slightly above room temperature (about 70–85°F) for about one hour before refrigerating. Dividing the soup into smaller containers will hasten the cooling process. I use inexpensive quart-size mason jars, but any heat-safe glass container will work (never use plastic containers for hot food, to avoid chemical leaching). Most chilled or puréed soups will last 2–3 days, refrigerated, and most stews will last about 4 days.

If you would like to stretch the lifespan of your soup even further, you can always freeze it! As with refrigerating, be sure you've brought the soup to a cool temperature before putting it in a container for freezing—in this case, a rapid temperature change can stress the material of your vessel and cause it to break.

Virtually any kind of soup can be frozen for months. Before reheating it, simply defrost the soup in the refrigerator for several hours or overnight. You may notice some subtle changes in the soup's texture or color (especially if it contains greens), but like most homemade superfood soups, it will retain 95 percent of its original delicious flavor…and every now and again actually be even better. Talk about a great ready-made meal!

HOW TO STRETCH YOUR SUPERFOOD SOUP BUDGET

Buy in season. Seasonal produce is always less expensive than produce purchased out of season (plus, seasonal items are often sold at discount prices, due to abundance). Not to mention, fresh produce picked at its peak tastes better, too. The recipes in these pages were written as a result of weekly trips to my local farmers market throughout the year, so you'll find a wide, exciting range of uses for nature's best-of-the-moment edibles.

Buy in bulk. Smart pantry staple purchases are the key to huge financial savings. If your supermarket has a bulk bin section, use it! If there are discounts on larger or multiple packages, take advantage of them! When kept in a cool, dark place in a sealed container (I often transfer them into airtight glass mason jars), pantry items will last months—even years—and will serve as the cornerstones of your soup making.

Let nothing go to waste. Most of the recipes in this book are designed to make quantities that four people might consume over the course of one meal. If you find yourself with leftovers and don't think you'll consume them within the next couple of days, you can freeze them for a later use. Also, look for ways to use up fresh produce in recipes. Soups are some of the most flexible recipes on the planet, so don't feel intimidated when it comes to adding a boost of, say, chopped fennel or an extra carrot if you find a homeless half veggie sitting in the refrigerator.

DIY. Your best bet for cost savings is to do as much soup making as you can. Simmering your own vegetable stock will be less expensive than buying a boxed variety. And, certainly, chopping your own vegetables instead of buying them pre-chopped in packages racks up enormous savings, fast.

CREATING A SUPERFOOD PANTRY STARTER KIT

Are you just starting out with your superfood pantry? No worries! There's no need to buy every single superfood overnight (unless of course, you want to, in which case, bravo!). While some people might jump into the world of superfoods full throttle, you may prefer to ease into it, and gradually add new things to your soup pot. If you're committed to truly enhancing your health and making a positive change, I suggest starting out with five superfoods. Once they've become a familiar part of your soup-making repertoire, you'll feel more comfortable about branching out and trying a few others. To get started on your healthy culinary journey, try these versatile, soup-friendly superfoods—you can use them in just about any kind of soup:

Goji berries (page 27)

Hemp seeds (page 33)

Maca powder (page 30)

Medicinal mushroom powder (pick one variety on page 18)

Dulse flakes (page 23)

THE NUTRITIONAL REWARDS OF SUPERFOOD SOUPS

Usually, when we're wondering, "What's for dinner?" most of us don't think too much beyond an option that sounds good. But there's another consideration that comes into play after you've eaten a delicious meal: how it interacts with and shapes your body. This consideration is the essence of conscious eating. It also plays into the concept of inner beauty—consuming foods that beautify our bones, organs, blood, and even our *cells*, creating an inner health environment so vibrant that it results in radiant outer beauty as well (makes sense, right?). The practice of supporting a healthy, balanced inner ecosystem creates a "best-ever" version of our bodies: we look good, and, even more important, we *feel* incredible. This is exactly what superfood soups are all about.

BUILT-IN BENEFITS

As you've read in the Superfood Soup Essentials section (page 16), every superfood has its own specific benefits. But beyond these individual ingredient traits, there are some real-deal advantages to enjoying superfood soup recipes on a regular basis.

Energy. We don't often think of sitting down to a big meal as something that will make us feel invigorated, but that's precisely what superfood soups do. Between the alkaline proteins and the high fiber and water they provide, you get a tried-and-true, easy-to-digest combo that makes it simpler for your body to break down nutrients and put them to use. Think of it this way: each day you spend about 10 percent of your energy just on digesting the food you eat. What if you could get a little of that energy back? You'd have more energy left to spend.

Minerals and Vitamins. When you look at "enriched" products on the shelf, whether it's flour, milk, juice, or whatever, what you're actually getting is added (and perhaps synthesized) vitamins and minerals. Unfortunately, our bodies have a very difficult time processing artificially supplemented forms of most nutrients, and many actually pass through the body undigested. The reason why this "enrichment" is needed in the first place is because so many of us struggle to meet our body's daily mineral requirements: whether it's due to nutrient loss in agricultural soils, or simply a matter of not eating enough mineral-rich foods, nutrient deficiencies are a frequent problem.

To help you meet your mineral needs naturally, easily, and deliciously, superfood soups pack in just about every alkaline, mineral-packed food under the sun, including roots, tubers, sea vegetables, seeds, grains, and greens.

Not to be outdone, vitamins are also a strong component of superfood soups, which is certainly something not every soup on the shelf can boast! Most recipes are created solely around flavor (that's why some restaurant chefs use butter like it's going out of style), without regard for what the process of cooking does to food—or how it affects us biologically. With this in mind, it's safe to say that most commercial vegetable soups are not particularly strong in the vitamin department, because most vitamins the ingredients may have originally contained get cooked away, if they were even there in the first place. Superfood soups, on the other hand, are designed to actually maximize nutritional gains. Delicate foods like leafy greens are usually added at the end of cooking in order to preserve their vitamin content as much as possible, and many stir-ins and toppings contain extra shots of vitamin-rich ingredients, so you'll get the healing benefits of vitamins with every spoonful.

Protective and Healing Antioxidants. No other foods on the planet can compete with superfoods in the antioxidant department. (In some cases, it's actually a food's exceptionally high antioxidant content alone that qualifies it as a superfood.) These antioxidants are responsible for protecting and healing our bodies from sickness and disease, and are present in massive quantities in superfood soup ingredients.

Antioxidants, famous for helping to prevent and fight cancer, also strengthen the body in myriad other ways, from soothing sore joints to boosting brainpower. Because of the abundance of antioxidants in superfood soups, it's almost tempting to call them a form of "everyday medicine," although the name doesn't do justice to how amazingly delicious they are!

ALKALINE VERSUS ACID FOODS

The pH balance in your body is one of the most vital aspects of your internal chemistry. Your body needs—and it's designed—to maintain a slightly alkaline (basic) blood pH, but it is constantly in a state of minute fluctuation, influenced by everything from normal body functions to the food you eat. Eating more alkaline foods (like plants, and particularly vegetables) means less strain on your body to maintain its optimal equilibrium and function efficiently.

BONUS BENEFITS

Although all the soups in this book confer a wealth of healthy nutritional advantages, each recipe offers a unique set of additional functional benefits, as well. If you're looking to utilize superfood soups to help address a specific health concern, such as bone strength or heart health, for example, simply look for the corresponding icons, below, to help you identify exactly which soups best suit your needs. For a list of recipes grouped by health benefit, please refer to the Soups by Benefit Index, starting on page 223.

BEAUTY   Soup contains ingredients that boast notable quantities of "beauty nutrients," such as vitamin C (for collagen production), important fats, and anti-inflammatory antioxidants for skin protection.

BONE STRENGTH   Soup abounds in calcium-rich superfoods.

CLEANSE/DETOX   Soup contains ingredients helpful in gently removing toxins from the body, while, at the same time, offering valuable micronutrients for biological renewal.

HEART HEALTH   Soup includes nutrients that have been shown, in clinical trials, to promote cardiovascular health.

IMMUNITY   Soup provides nutrients that fight disease—such as vitamin C and zinc—and/or contains superfoods renowned for their antiviral, antibacterial, or antifungal properties.

LOW CALORIE   Soup contains approximately 250 calories or less per serving.

PROTEIN   Soup has 6 grams of protein or more per serving.

USING SUPERFOOD SOUPS TO RESET YOUR DIET (SOUP CLEANSING, AKA "SOUPING")

"Not again!" That's how I felt. I had planned on having a very healthy winter holiday while visiting my in-laws in Germany, but my lovely family thwarted me. I'm usually pretty "good" while traveling: I eat lots of local fruit and vegetables, and even bring some of my superfood insurance (packets of green powder, a couple of bags of goji berries, and smoothie mixes) just to be on the safe side. But, upon my arrival, I was met with stacks of dark chocolate, beautiful European fruit breads, and found bowls filled with little bites of sweetness that whispered "eat me" everywhere I turned. In those six glorious days, my schedule was pretty intense: eating great food, lying around, and eating great food. As you can imagine, it was a wonderful trip.

But, of course, this is not exactly a sustainable lifestyle! When I got back home, I didn't just want to make a smoothie and move on; I needed to give my body a real factory reset. And since it was winter, I turned to warm soups. My "reset" was easy: I made a few big batches of cleansing superfood soups—actually, this is how the recipe for Many Greens Soup (page 107) first came about—and enjoyed them, over the course of a few days, along with a couple of other healthy eats, such as salads and the like. Not only was this an easy regimen (2 hours of cooking yielded days and days worth of meals), I was also impressed by how absolutely amazing I felt after devoting such a short amount

of time to it! I love fresh-pressed juices for cleansing (one look at my book *Superfood Juices* will tell you that), but the difference was that whereas juices are energizing and light, soups are energizing and *deeply satisfying* over the long term. I was in love with how revitalized I felt: fueled but not full, and consistently invigorated.

It turns out there's a name for this practice of eating soups as a means of healthy realignment: it's simply called *souping*. It is considered, by many, to be the smartest way to "cleanse," because eating nutrient-dense soups made with whole, unprocessed foods enriches your body with everything it needs while keeping hunger at bay. While I tend to shy away from diet trends faster than you can say "the Master Cleanse" (the lemonade diet—what?!), souping actually makes a whole lot of sense because it doesn't deprive you of anything. In fact, it does just the opposite: souping satisfies your entire body with deeply efficient nourishment.

The moral here is that maintaining an overall balance in what you eat over the course of your lifetime is ideal. But sometimes, when you need to regain that balance…to energize, heal, and glow from within again, a few days of souping might just be the answer. While all of the soups in this book can be used for this purpose, recipes with the Cleanse/Detox symbol 🍃 will be the most effective (for a full list of cleansing and detoxing soups, see page 223).

PART TWO

THE SOUPS

Soup is a little bit magical. This flexible medium, with its endless variations and possibilities, acts as an open invitation to just about any natural ingredient, interesting vegetable, or exotic spice. There's a dramatically diverse range of soup flavors and styles in these pages to satisfy all kinds of taste: you can enjoy the full flavors of a fresh, healing stock in the Rejuvenating Broths section; tantalize your taste buds with the pleasures of Chilled & Light Soups; melt away in the velvety bliss of Smooth & Creamy Soups; revel in the earnest comforts of Brothy & Noodle Soups; luxuriate in luscious Chowders & Porridges; or go all-out hearty with generously composed Stews & Chilis. Whatever your mood, superfood soups offer the promise of energizing comfort with each delicious spoonful.

BEFORE YOU BEGIN

There is no recipe for homemade soup in this world that does not occasionally require slight adjustments, as there are many variables at work! First, aside from your individual taste for salt, spice, and so on, the quality of natural foods can vary widely, depending on the crop itself...the batch of spice...or even the season. More important, the flavor of a finished soup will inevitably change slightly as it sits and cools. Some of these changes might be more beneficial than others. For example, the flavors of a stew-like soup might meld and bloom more fully with an extra hour (or more) of sitting, whereas a pungent soup might not fare as well if it loses its "kick" (or acid) with time. To counter this unpredictability, there is one sure rule: *taste before serving*. I encourage you to feel confident about tweaking the recipes in this book as your personal taste dictates. To best achieve the flavors you desire, use the following secrets to ensure that every batch you make is superb.

SOUP FINISHING TIPS

Too bland? Add salt and pepper.
More often than not, a too-bland soup is the result of not using enough classic seasoning (aka salt and pepper)—usually salt. Stir in a pinch at a time, taste, and bring the soup to a level that is just right for you. Salt and pepper may be the most important (and underappreciated!) spices we have: they bring flavor to life.

Too flat? Add acid.
Sometimes, a soup can taste a little flat, especially if it has been sitting for a period of time. Adding a spoonful of an acidic ingredient, such as lemon or lime juice, or any kind of vinegar, can often lift and lighten heavy flavors and add the pep that a soup needs.

Too thick? Add water.
A soup that's on the thick side (often the result of stock or water that has simply evaporated a little too quickly) can easily be remedied by adding water. Simply stir in about ¼ cup of water at a time, until the soup has the desired consistency. You can use other liquids, too, but be aware that they will affect the flavor of the soup. When reheating a soup that was made days or even hours previously, you may need to add a little extra water or stock to loosen the ingredients.

Too thin? Keep cooking...or add arrowroot.
There are several remedies for a soup that's too brothy (too thin) for your liking. The first is to simply cook the soup a little longer, to allow more moisture to evaporate. If you're short on time, or

run the risk of overcooking more delicate vegetables, the second method is to simply add an ingredient that absorbs moisture, such as a little wheat flour (a common solution). However, I'm a much bigger fan of using arrowroot powder, which is drastically more efficient than flour and actually lends a slightly smooth and creamy texture to soup without influencing the flavor. The trick is to just use a little—1 teaspoon up to 1 tablespoon of arrowroot will likely be enough. Whisk it into a little warm broth, then stir this slurry into the soup, and continue to cook the soup for a couple of minutes to let it thicken. If the soup is still not thick enough, add more arrowroot as needed. I always keep a jar of arrowroot powder in my pantry as a just-in-case ingredient—it lasts an exceptionally long time!

BLENDING SOUPS SAFELY

Hot soups produce lots of steam, which in turn creates a tremendous amount of pressure, especially when it's trapped inside the vortex of a sealed, whirring blender. When puréeing hot liquids and soup, it's important to take a few precautions to avoid literally blowing off the lid. First, if your blender has a removable cap on the lid, remove it before blending, cover the gap with a paper towel, and hold down the lid with a cloth towel on top. Blend slowly at first, release a little of the hot air, then cover the blender again and blend until smooth. The second trick is to simply not fill the blender all the way—I usually stop at three quarters of the way full, to allow plenty of room for the expansion of hot air while the soup is being processed.

Prep thoroughly. All your ingredients should be prepped and ready to go before you start to make a recipe: chop the onions; blend the spices; make sure you have enough vegetable stock. Some soup recipes need to come together rather quickly and rely on a cooking flow that can only be achieved when all ingredients are *mise en place*, or put in place, as the French say. Pretend you are a line cook, getting ready for the grand entrance of the head chef!

Pay attention to chop sizes. The majority of soup recipes are pretty relaxed, but paying special attention to your knife skills during prep (keeping chop sizes fairly consistent) will guarantee a better soup, because your ingredients will cook at the same rate. Also, at the risk of sounding like an overprotective parent, I have to add that it's super important to keep your chopping simple and *safe*. Cut large items, like squashes and tubers, into manageable pieces before chopping finely, and create flat edges to keep produce from rolling around while slicing. For example, cut a potato quickly by simply halving or quartering it before slicing it, cutting it into rectangular strips, then chopping the strips into even dice.

Get that pot nice and hot. Always make sure the oil in the pot is hot (but never smoking) before adding ingredients. To test if the oil is hot enough, toss in a piece of chopped onion and watch how it reacts when it hits the surface of the oil. If the onion sizzles, your pot is ready to go. If it does nothing, wait another minute before trying again. A nice layer of properly seared vegetables and their juices can do wonders for enhancing the flavor of soup.

Season a little as you go—but mostly at the end of cooking. Soups need a little bit of salt and pepper action while they're cooking to help draw out flavor, but the best time to add seasoning is toward the end of cooking, when you can get a full sense of the finished recipe. In truth, you can achieve the best results by following your own intuition when it comes to seasoning soup.

Play with garnish. Soups bring out the artist in all of us. Let your inner creativity shine as you garnish your soup with different colors, textures, and superfoods!

For superfood ingredient substitutions, see page 217. Resources can be found on page 219.

REJUVENATING BROTHS

With one sip of their enchantingly deep flavors and profoundly warming attributes, you too will become a convert to savory homemade broths. These infusions, made from vegetables and superfoods, serve several purposes. A recipe like Miso Broth, for example, serves as the backbone for many soups, offering a depth of flavor that's as important as the box spring is to your mattress. Other recipes, such as Beauty Broth, are medicinal sipping broths that support a radiant body from the inside out. Each of these easy broths, whether it's a simple spin on a classic recipe or something a little more exotic, provides a very special superfood touch.

= FEATURED SUPERFOOD INGREDIENT

BEAUTY   BONE STRENGTH   CLEANSE/DETOX

HEART HEALTH   IMMUNITY   LOW CALORIE   PROTEIN

WHY MAKE BROTH?

Should we meet, I think you and I would get along nicely, because anyone who reads the broth section of a soup cookbook—and takes it seriously—is definitely a like-minded foodie soul. Most people take soup broths for granted, assuming that they are little more than glorified water. But broths and stocks are the hardest-working, most underappreciated members of the soup world. Although they are always in the background of "celebrity" soup ingredients, don't be fooled: broths make the secret difference between a good soup and a great soup.

Even so, I know what you're thinking. I, too, have often passed up a chef's suggestion that I make a broth for a soup recipe ("Let's be real: you're telling me I need to make *two* soups?") and have just used water or a ready-made variety instead. While it's perfectly okay to use a good-quality store-bought broth for any recipe in this book, I would like to offer a compelling reason to make your own: a bonus layer of superfoods! Yes, the broths you'll find here are in fact superfood

broths, and each is extra packed with incredible benefits.

These amazing broths are the epitome of easy, and not much more complicated to make than tea (albeit a slow-cooked tea). Each recipe makes 8–12 cups of broth, but if you have more than one pot that's big enough, I highly recommend making even larger batches.

USING SUPERFOOD BROTHS

The broth recipes in this book are all nutrient-dense, plant-based broths, but you can use them for all types of soup recipes—even ones that call for chicken, beef, or fish stock. Here's a quick plant-based substitution guide:

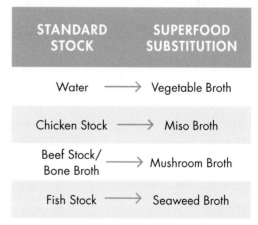

STANDARD STOCK	SUPERFOOD SUBSTITUTION
Water	→ Vegetable Broth
Chicken Stock	→ Miso Broth
Beef Stock/ Bone Broth	→ Mushroom Broth
Fish Stock	→ Seaweed Broth

TIP: Freeze your broths! While most broths will last about 1 week in the refrigerator, they can also be stored in sealed containers for months at a time in the freezer, ready to be used whenever the soup spirit moves you. Instead of freezing stocks in jars, use shallow glass food containers—they thaw much more quickly when you defrost them.

CULINARY BROTHS

Culinary broths serve two purposes: to sip as a warm drink, much as you would enjoy a hot cup of savory tea, but even more so, to use as essential ingredients in many of the soup recipes in this book.

Culinary broths serve two purposes: to sip as a warm drink, much as you would enjoy a hot cup of savory tea, but even more so, to use as essential ingredients in many of the soup recipes in this book.

Culinary broths serve two purposes: to sip as a warm drink, much as you would enjoy a hot cup of savory tea, but even more so, to use as essential ingredients in many of the soup recipes in this book.

VEGETABLE BROTH

This is a blond broth, with a flavor that dances between savory and delicately sweet, with an energizing boost of maca root. I will often make this broth and end up drinking a piping-hot mugful before it even makes it into a soup recipe! I use my favorite vegetables in this recipe to get the flavor I love most, but feel free to do the same and swap in your own favorites. See Vegetable Broth 101 (on the next page) for more ideas.

MAKES ABOUT 3 QUARTS (12 CUPS)

4 large onions (any variety)

2 tsp olive oil

3 Tbsp red wine vinegar

2 medium leeks, white and green parts cleaned and chopped

1 medium celery root, peeled and chopped

1 large (or 2 small) fennel bulbs, chopped

4 carrots, chopped

2 Tbsp maca powder

¼ cup whole fresh thyme (leaves and stems)

1 Tbsp whole black peppercorns

5 quarts water

Slice two of the onions in half and remove only the most papery skin. Slice each half into quarters, while keeping the half together as a unit. Set the cut halves aside. Chop the remaining two onions into smaller pieces and keep them on standby with the other chopped vegetables.

In a big stockpot,* warm the olive oil over medium heat. Carefully place the sliced onion halves, cut side down, in the oil. Cook for 10 minutes to sear and deeply brown the bottoms—don't stir or disturb the onions while they are cooking. Add the vinegar and quickly stir together with the onions to deglaze the bottom of the pot. Add all the remaining ingredients, in the order that they are listed, and turn the heat up to bring the mixture to a boil. Reduce the heat to a simmer, and cook for 45 minutes to 1 hour, skimming the top as necessary to remove any foam. Strain the broth, cool, and store.

Broth may be stored in the refrigerator for up to 1 week, or kept in the freezer for several months.

* The minimum size of pot you'll need is 8 quarts, although 10 quarts or larger would be a more comfortable fit for this broth. If you don't have a big enough pot, divide the recipe between two pots, amounting to 8–12 quarts altogether.

VEGETABLE BROTH 101

Vegetable broths are arguably the most diverse broths of all. Use these tips to make your own special varieties!

Use (almost) any vegetable. For a balanced flavor, you'll still want to start out with a basic mirepoix—onions, celery, and carrots (or some similar combination of veggies)—but from there, the additions are almost endless, including all kinds of roots and tubers, like turnips and parsnips, and bulbous aromatics, like fennel and garlic. The exceptions to this free-spirited mix are few, but do avoid cruciferous vegetables like cabbage and cauliflower, as their flavors can be overwhelmingly strong, as well as delicate vegetables, like lettuce and other leafy greens, whose nutrition will get lost in the cooking process.

Add spices. Most conventional broths are light on herbs and spices in order to provide a base that can be used in a variety of recipes. But if you're making your own (for sipping or a particular soup), adding additional spices is extremely rewarding. Common seasonings include fresh herbs, bay leaves, peppercorns, and dried whole spices. Other broths may include special ingredients such as ginger, lemongrass, turmeric, and medicinal mushroom powders.

Keep it easy with chopping. One of the nice things about making a broth is that it doesn't involve a lot of chopping! You can almost get away with throwing whole vegetables into a pot. But making at least a small effort to chop them into a few pieces will cut down on cooking time as well as increase the amount of flavor that the vegetables infuse into the broth. At the very least, most vegetables should be quartered, although you can certainly chop them into smaller pieces if you like.

Use produce "waste." Broth is an excellent way to combat vegetable waste in the kitchen. To make a broth, you can use all kinds of things, such as papery onion skins, leek greens, extra trimmings from carrots and celery, and even vegetable peels that would normally be discarded, even though they still have plenty of flavor to offer. However, this does not mean that your broth should be entirely composed of these extraneous ingredients: consider them as add-ins that should not make up more than one-third of your ingredient list. Also, be sure to clean them very well, and never use old produce that's too deteriorated to eat.

Add salt. Salting broth is a purely preferential activity. If you decide to season with salt and are experimenting with a new recipe, wait until the very end—after you've strained the ingredients—to avoid creating a mixture that's overly salty (broth boils down and condenses quite a lot while cooking).

MUSHROOM BROTH

Mushroom broth adds an immensely earthy flavor to hearty soups and stews, and although you can buy premade mushroom broths at the store, it's incredibly satisfying to make your own, using the best mushrooms you can find. This recipe, like the one for Vegetable Broth (page 60), is very flexible: use whatever variety of dried mushrooms you like (or a blend of dry and fresh mushrooms is great, too—wild mushrooms taste pretty outstanding, I must say) and add your favorite powdered superfood mushrooms. Dried mushrooms are not only less expensive than fresh mushrooms, but they're also ideal for broths, since their flavor intensifies (much like tea leaves) as they steep. I like to keep things simple by not going crazy with herbs and seasonings in this broth, which keeps it the most flexible for use in a variety of soup recipes. Nevertheless, consider this a base recipe, and feel free to bump up the flavor even further by adding extra flavorings like a few sprigs of thyme, rosemary, bay leaves, or additional vegetables like leek greens, fennel, or celery root.

MAKES ABOUT 10 CUPS

1 large yellow onion, peeled and quartered

4 garlic cloves, smashed and peeled

1 carrot, quartered

1 stalk celery, quartered

1 oz dried mushrooms (any variety)

1 Tbsp superfood mushroom powder (any variety, such as cordyceps, reishi, chaga, or a blend)

½ tsp sea salt

1 gallon (16 cups) water

Warm a large, heavy-bottomed pot over medium heat. Once it is hot, dry cook the onions for 5 minutes (do not stir or move the onions while they are cooking) to caramelize the bottoms.

Add the remaining ingredients and bring to a boil, then reduce the heat to a low simmer. Cook the broth for about 1 hour, or until the mixture has reduced almost by half. Turn off the heat, cover, and let the broth sit at room temperature for 30 minutes to steep and cool. Drain the broth and store in the refrigerator for later use. Broth may be stored in the refrigerator for up to 1 week, or kept in the freezer for several months.

MISO BROTH

Here you have it: my absolute favorite simple soup broth, and the one you should definitely commit to memory. It's unbelievably versatile and easy to make, and it punches up the flavor of everything it's added to! Unlike most recipes for miso soups, which only gently warm the miso (traditionally, it's added at the end of a recipe to preserve its delicate enzymes), I treat this broth just like any other by adding it to soups early on. It's sacrilege, I know, to waste a few innocent enzymes, but in this instance it's really the flavor of miso that we're after.

There are infinite ways to punch up a miso broth, but this recipe is a great place to start. I like to use yellow miso paste here, as it's the most versatile, but feel free to substitute other varieties—white miso paste has the weakest flavor, while brown and red miso pastes are the strongest. If you're avoiding soy, chickpea miso is a great resource to use, too.

MAKES ABOUT 8 CUPS

4 Tbsp yellow miso paste

1 tsp kelp granules

2 quarts (8 cups) water

Blend all the ingredients together in a blender until the miso is fully dissolved. Use in soups as directed, or warm over low heat to enjoy as a sipping broth.

The broth may be stored in the refrigerator for up to 1 week, or kept in the freezer for several months.

FEEL-GOOD FACT: Broths containing seaweed, like kelp or kombu, are naturally high in minerals and electrolytes. Warmed up, they make an excellent post-exercise drink to aid in recovery and hydration.

SEAWEED BROTH

I feel like I could practically live off this broth: just one taste and it feels profoundly "right." It is truly loaded with minerals. You can swap another type of seaweed into this recipe (or use a combination of seaweed), but the tougher varieties, like kombu, will offer the best briny flavor without being too overwhelming. I've found that kombu is the most versatile seagreen to use in broths—there's a reason why it is at the base of so many classic Japanese recipes!

MAKES ABOUT 10 CUPS

3 quarts (12 cups) filtered water

1 piece dried kombu (about 2×4 inches)

2 Tbsp tamari

Bring the water to a boil in a large, heavy-bottomed pot. Add the kombu, and reduce the heat to medium-low. Partially cover and simmer for 30 minutes. Remove the kombu (save it for another use, if desired), and stir in the tamari. Let the broth cool a bit before transferring it to a storage container.

Seaweed Broth will last for 1 week in the refrigerator, or for several months in the freezer.

Superfood Tip: *Save that seaweed! Once the broth has finished cooking, remove the seaweed, let it cool, mince it into small pieces, and use it as a delicious and healthy addition to savory soups, salads, grain bowls, and more (note that after cooking, the seaweed won't have too much flavor but will still retain a small portion of its nutrition). As a last resort, you can use it as a natural dog treat—my dog gobbles it up like a favorite chew toy.*

WHY BONE BROTH IS NOT A SUPERFOOD

Bone broth is a dense broth made by slow-simmering animal bones (and sometimes extra parts, like feet and tendons) for extensive periods of time. Although bone broth has enjoyed a wave of popularity in recent years, it is nothing new—it has been used in soups around the world for centuries as a way to use up animal by-products and waste, and to promote health and healing. Now that bone broth is back in vogue, its advocates are making some very attractive health claims about the broth, including enhanced immunity, liver detoxification, better digestive health, younger skin, healthier joints—and it's even being used as a sports recovery drink.

These claims about bone broth have not come out of thin air. Bone broth is, in fact, a source of collagen—a protein that contains amino acids, which compose and repair connective tissues in joints, tendons, bone, and skin. In particular, bone broth contains glutamine, an amino acid that is responsible for many types of tissue repair and is particularly helpful in addressing digestive disorders, such as leaky gut syndrome. Bone broth also contains electrolytes, which are important for hydration after exercise.

While the nutritional value of bone broth is very real, many of the claims surrounding bone broth may not be. The inclusion of bone broth's most famous nutrient, collagen, is widely misrepresented. Your body can't simply digest the collagen from an animal and use it as collagen for your own joints and skin. Instead, your body breaks it down into individual amino acids, just like it would with any food, and uses them wherever they are needed in the body's ecosystem (hint: collagen production is usually not the first in line). In truth, it's not the collagen in bone broth, but rather the individual amino acids, which abound in nutrient-dense foods of all kinds, such as hemp seeds, goji berries, seaweed, and more, that are important. Also, it should be noted that the human body makes collagen on its own, and many experts suggest that if you really want to build collagen, it's much more effective to consume supportive micronutrients and antioxidants, like vitamin C and lycopene (which are not contained in bone broth) that are extremely efficient in rebuilding collagen. In fact, there is nothing special in bone broth that is not easily sourced in quantity from other foods in the natural food kingdom, and obtained through a whole food, plant-based diet...particularly one that is rich in superfoods.

But the most serious concerns about bone broth go beyond the claims of its most vocal promoters. For one, the quality of commercial bone broth varies wildly: you don't know where the boiled animal parts really came from or what they are, for that matter. You also don't know what the animal(s) were fed, what their environment and living conditions were like, or if they were exposed to hormones. Additionally, heavy metals accrue in the bones, ligaments, and skin of mature animals, and this is exactly what is leached into the broth after hours of boiling. In fact, a 2013 blind study, published in *Medical Hypotheses*, showed that organic chicken bone broth contained "markedly high lead concentrations" (a highly dangerous neurotoxin). Conversely, there has not been a single positive study that definitively links bone broth to any of its proponents' claims of joint protection, stronger bones, and looking younger.

In place of bone broth, I highly suggest using the effective plant-based healing broths and soups in this book. Every nutrient found in bone broth can easily be found in much healthier, safer, and well-studied plant foods, from collagen-building nutrients (like those in leafy greens and sea vegetables) and joint-healthy glutamine (found in legumes, mushrooms, and raw vegetables) to electrolytes (such as those in chia seeds and celery). Eating true superfood soups and broths is a real food, risk-free plan that will support your body on absolutely every level.

BROTHS VERSUS STOCKS

Although the words are used interchangeably, there is a difference between a broth and a stock. A broth can be enjoyed either as-is (for sipping out of a mug) or used as an ingredient in another recipe, while a stock is just an ingredient to be used in the production of other dishes and is generally not enjoyed on its own.

FUNCTIONAL BROTHS

Broths have been used over the millennia as an effective method of delivering remedial nutrients. It's easy to make big batches of these potent functional broths, each of which (as the name suggests) is specially crafted to serve your needs, whether it's enhanced energy, detox, beauty, or healing. Although you can certainly use these functional recipes to make other soups, they are best enjoyed on their own. I often find myself reaching for a second or even third mug of broth throughout the day, particularly when a fresh batch is around—it just makes me feel incredible.

ENERGY BROTH

Experience a warm energy drink that goes way beyond a cup of coffee—energy that comes through nourishment, rather than stimulation, and provides a boost that you can feel long-term (and without a crash, later). This broth works with your body on every level, from supplying electrolytes for cellular recovery, B vitamins for energy, phytochemicals for adrenal support (which help with stress management), and even functional ingredients like cordyceps and cayenne that help boost circulation for maximum nutrient absorption.

MAKES ABOUT 10 CUPS / 8 SERVINGS

2 onions (any variety)

2 Tbsp coconut oil

4 carrots, coarsely chopped

4 stalks celery, coarsely chopped

2 Tbsp apple cider vinegar

2 bags green tea

✳ 2 Tbsp maca powder

✳ 2 Tbsp cordyceps powder

1 tsp whole peppercorns

⅛ tsp cayenne pepper

¾ tsp sea salt

1 gallon (16 cups) water

1 Tbsp nutritional yeast

Wash the whole onions, and then slice them in half, leaving the peel intact.

In a big stockpot, warm the coconut oil over medium heat. Carefully place the sliced onion halves, cut side down, in the oil. Add the carrots and celery, and cook them for 10 minutes to sear and deeply brown the bottoms—don't stir or disturb the vegetables while they are cooking. Add the vinegar and quickly stir the contents of the pan with the vinegar to deglaze the bottom of the pot. Add all the remaining ingredients, except the nutritional yeast, and turn the heat up to a boil. Reduce the heat to a simmer, and cook the mixture for 45 minutes to 1 hour (to desired concentration). Strain the broth into a bowl or pitcher, discarding the solids. Stir in the nutritional yeast. Working in batches, transfer the mixture to a blender and blend briefly to emulsify. Enjoy it as a warm sipping broth.

The broth may be stored in the refrigerator for up to 1 week and reheated, as needed, or kept in the freezer for months.

Note: This recipe may also be used in place of regular vegetable broth in other recipes.

DETOX BROTH

The subject of detoxification is admittedly a bit undermined these days by overuse in health circles. But, at its core, there is still an ocean of validity behind its simple but important use: helping the body to effectively release toxins that accrue in the body through everyday living. This broth does just that: it's a gentle diuretic that encourages healthy cellular function, and includes one of the most powerful detoxification tools on the planet: brown seaweed (kelp). Don't just do "a cleanse"—infuse your lifestyle with healthy practices, such as sipping one or two cups of this lemongrass-flavored broth.

MAKES ABOUT 8 CUPS / 6 SERVINGS

2 leeks

3 stalks fresh lemongrass

4 stalks celery, coarsely chopped

2 carrots, coarsely chopped

2 cloves garlic, peeled and smashed

2 inches fresh ginger root, sliced thin

1 cup mushrooms (any variety), halved

2 tsp kelp powder

2 bags cleansing tea*

½ bunch parsley

1 handful fresh mint

12 cups water

2 Tbsp yellow miso paste

2 tsp coconut oil

Trim the roots and any compromised tips from the leeks and discard. Slice the leeks to separate the white bulb from the greens. Slice both sides of the leek in half, and wash them thoroughly (leeks can be sandy). For the lemongrass, cut off and discard the tough tops and root ends, and then remove the coarse outer layers. Crush the inner part of the lemongrass with the flat side of a large knife, just as you would smash a clove of garlic.

In a big stockpot, add all the ingredients except the miso paste and coconut oil. Bring the mixture to a boil over high heat, and then reduce the heat to medium-low and simmer for 40–50 minutes (to desired concentration). Strain the broth into a bowl or pitcher, discarding the solids. Stir in the miso paste and coconut oil. Working in batches, transfer the mixture to a blender and blend to emulsify. Enjoy it as a warm sipping broth.

The broth may be stored in the refrigerator for up to 1 week and reheated as needed, or kept in the freezer for months.

* There are lots of different cleansing teas on the market. You can use pure nettle tea, dandelion tea, or a blend of herbal ingredients such as nettles, fennel, and mint in this recipe—just be sure the tea is not flavored with sweet spices like cinnamon, or the taste will be affected.

BEAUTY BROTH

Don't let the classic tomato-basil flavor of this broth fool you into thinking that it's "just" a delicious soup: it has some incredible beautifying powers, fueled by anti-aging antioxidants in green tea, goji berries, carrots, and tomatoes; anti-bacterial properties in garlic and basil (very helpful for clear skin); and youth-protective ALA and zinc in hemp seed oil. An overall great source of electrolyte-packed hydration, this broth is a wonderful way to enjoy some of nature's best beauty nutrients.

MAKES ABOUT 10 CUPS / 8 SERVINGS

2 onions (any variety)

1 tsp olive oil

3 stalks celery, coarsely chopped

2 carrots, coarsely chopped

3 Tbsp apple cider vinegar

1 Tbsp tomato paste

3 cloves garlic, peeled and smashed

1 gallon (16 cups) water

2 bags green tea

1 large handful fresh basil

¼ cup dried goji berries

2 Tbsp hemp oil

4 Tbsp yellow miso paste

Wash the whole onions, then slice them in half, leaving the peel intact.

In a big stockpot, warm the olive oil over medium heat, letting it spread over the bottom of the pan. Carefully place the sliced onion halves, cut side down, into the pan. Add the carrots and celery, and cook for 10 minutes to sear and deeply brown their bottoms—don't stir or disturb the vegetables while they are cooking. Add the vinegar and quickly stir the contents of the pan with the vinegar to deglaze the bottom of the pot. Stir in the tomato paste and garlic, and then add the water, green tea bags, and whole basil. Turn the heat up to bring the broth to a boil. Reduce the heat to a simmer, and cook the mixture for 45 minutes to 1 hour (to desired concentration). Strain the broth into a bowl or pitcher, discarding the solids. Stir in the goji berries, hemp oil, and miso paste. Working in batches, transfer the mixture to a blender and blend until smooth. Enjoy it as a warm sipping broth.

The broth may be stored in the refrigerator for up to 1 week and reheated as needed, or kept in the freezer for months.

HEALING BROTH

For all intents and purposes, this slightly spicy, turmeric-rich broth could be classified solely as a cold- and flu-fighting soup (in the world of naturopathic medicine, the ingredients are considered to be a great support to the immune system), yet there's more to this recipe than just that. Thanks to an abundance of anti-inflammatory nutrients and antioxidants, sourced from some of the most powerful restorative superfoods on the planet like turmeric, reishi, and goji, this broth is truly healing—it's an excellent tool for overall repair and recovery from all types of stresses, diseases, and injuries. Use it regularly or whenever you're in need of some mending TLC.

MAKES ABOUT 10 CUPS / 8 SERVINGS

2 yellow onions

2 Tbsp coconut oil, divided

2 stalks celery, quartered

2 carrots, quartered

3 Tbsp apple cider vinegar

1 gallon (16 cups) water

4 cloves garlic, peeled and smashed

2 inches fresh ginger root, sliced

1 tsp ground turmeric

1 Tbsp reishi mushroom powder

1 tsp black peppercorns

⅛ tsp cayenne powder, or more to taste

⅓ cup dried goji berries

3 Tbsp yellow miso paste

Wash the whole onions, and then slice them in half, leaving the peel intact.

In a big stockpot, warm 1 tablespoon of the coconut oil over medium heat, allowing it to spread over the bottom surface of the pan. Carefully place the sliced onion halves, cut side down, in the oil. Add the celery and carrots, and cook them for 10 minutes to sear and deeply brown the bottoms—don't stir or disturb the vegetables while they are cooking. Add the vinegar and quickly stir the contents of the pan with the vinegar to deglaze the bottom of the pot. Add the water, garlic, ginger, turmeric, reishi, peppercorns, and cayenne. Turn the heat up to high and bring the mixture to a boil. Reduce the heat to a simmer, and cook for 1 hour. Strain the broth into a bowl or pitcher, discarding the solids. Stir in the goji berries, miso paste, and remaining 1 tablespoon of coconut oil. Working in batches, transfer the mixture to a blender and blend until smooth. Enjoy it as a warm sipping broth.

The broth may be stored in the refrigerator for up to 1 week and reheated as needed, or kept in the freezer for months.

CHILLED SOUPS

Chilled soups are utterly lovely. These recipes, usually served at the start of a meal (although they're hearty enough to be a light lunch unto themselves), are the perfect way to cool down and enjoy superfood soups during the warmer months. To take advantage of treasured hot-weather produce, try making seasonal delicacies like Goldenberry Peach Gazpacho (page 82), which explodes with sweet-sour goldenberry flavor and vitamin C from camu berries, or relax with an easy Watercress Vichyssoise (page 75), a peppery, leafy green soup that's a pleasurable meal in a cup.

✳ = FEATURED SUPERFOOD INGREDIENT

✳ BEAUTY   ⬡ BONE STRENGTH   🌿 CLEANSE/DETOX

♥ HEART HEALTH   ✳ IMMUNITY   💧 LOW CALORIE   ⬡ PROTEIN

WATERCRESS VICHYSSOISE

Vichyssoise is a classic French soup, traditionally made of puréed leeks, onions, potatoes, chicken broth, and cream. This plant-based version capitalizes on watercress and a little fennel to give the soothing base a delightfully fresh and subtle peppery edge.

MAKES 8 CUPS / 6 SERVINGS

1 Tbsp olive oil, plus extra for garnish

1 large leek, white and light green parts only, sliced thin

½ yellow onion, finely chopped

1 medium bulb fennel (½ lb), diced, plus a few fronds for garnish

1 lb russet potatoes, peeled and cut into ½-inch dice

1 tsp fennel seeds

1 tsp minced fresh thyme

5 cups Vegetable Broth (page 60, or store bought)

Sea salt and ground black pepper

¼ cup raw cashews

1 bunch watercress (about 3 cups packed), trimmed

Warm the oil in a heavy-bottomed pot over medium-low heat. Add the leek, onion, and fennel, and sweat for 3–4 minutes, or until the vegetables begin to turn translucent. Add the potatoes, fennel seeds, thyme, broth, a pinch of salt, and ½ teaspoon ground pepper, and increase the heat to high. Bring to a boil, and then reduce the heat to medium-low. Simmer until the potatoes are very soft, about 25–30 minutes. Remove from the heat and add the cashews and watercress. Working in batches if needed, transfer the soup to a blender, and purée until smooth, adding a little water to thin, if needed. Adjust salt and pepper to taste. Refrigerate the soup for about 2 hours to chill and serve with a light drizzle of olive oil and a couple of fennel fronds on top.

Variation: *Although vichyssoise is traditionally served cold, you can also serve it warm. Try gently heating the soup over low heat until it is warmed through. You can even stir in 2–3 cups of cooked quinoa for an extra-hearty meal.*

AVOCADO NORI SOUP WITH CRISPY RICE

This Asian-inspired soup is so easy and fast, it almost qualifies as an instant soup. To make it into a heartier dish, simply spoon a serving of brown rice or quinoa into a bowl and ladle the soup on top of it. While this soup recipe makes a quick and easy lunch, it also doubles as a great appetizer.

MAKES 4 CUPS / 4 SERVINGS

2 nori sheets

1 cup mashed avocado (about 2 medium or 1 large)

3 cups water

1 Tbsp yellow miso paste

1½ tsp rice wine vinegar

½ cup unsweetened crispy brown rice cereal

¼ cup toasted sesame seeds

Over a wide bowl, crumble the nori sheets with your hands, crushing them into small pieces. Add half of the nori to a blender, and reserve the other half for garnish. Add the avocado, water, miso paste, and rice wine vinegar to the blender, and purée until smooth. Taste for seasoning, and adjust miso (for salt) or vinegar (for acid), if desired. Place in the refrigerator until chilled, or about 30 minutes. Pour into serving bowls and top with the remaining nori, crispy brown rice, and a sprinkle of sesame seeds.

SUPERFOOD BOOST: Add 1 teaspoon spirulina powder to the ingredients before blending. Spirulina will give the soup a slightly darker green color, but it won't change the flavor. It will, however, add extra minerals and immune-boosting nutrients.

YOGURT-CUCUMBER SOUP WITH HARISSA-ROASTED GARBANZO BEANS

I could quite happily eat this soup every day during the summer—it's an amazingly rich (yet light!) starter soup that seems to go with everything, and once the roasted garbanzo beans are made, can easily be assembled right before serving.

MAKES 5 CUPS/ 4 SERVINGS

1½ cups cooked garbanzo beans (page 13, or 1 15-oz can, drained)

3 Tbsp Goji Harissa (page 206), or store-bought harissa, divided

Sea salt and ground black pepper

2 cups unsweetened coconut-milk yogurt (or plain nondairy yogurt of choice), divided

2 cups finely chopped Persian (small) cucumbers (about 1 lb)

½ tsp wheatgrass powder (optional)

2 Tbsp minced fresh mint, plus extra leaves, for garnish

1 Tbsp fresh lemon juice

Water

Preheat the oven to 400°F. Line a baking sheet with a silicone baking mat or parchment paper.

Wash the garbanzo beans, then rub them inside a clean cloth kitchen towel to dry them very thoroughly. Transfer the beans to a bowl, and discard any bean skins that have come loose. Add 2 tablespoons of harissa paste along with a pinch of salt and pepper, and mix well to coat the beans evenly. Spread the beans on the prepared baking sheet, and place it in the oven. Bake the beans for 25–30 minutes, giving them a toss every 8 minutes or so, or until the beans are lightly browned and a little crispy on the outside. Remove the beans from the oven and let them cool.

While the beans are roasting, make the soup. In a blender, add the yogurt, cucumber, wheatgrass, mint, lemon juice, and ½ teaspoon sea salt. Blend for just a moment—soup should retain a little bit of texture from the cucumber. Place in the refrigerator and chill until ready to use.

To serve, spoon the last 1 tablespoon of harissa into a small bowl, and whisk in a dash of water—about a teaspoon or two—to slightly loosen the paste. Pour the soup into bowls, and generously drizzle the tops with the remaining harissa. Use the back of a knife or a toothpick to decoratively swirl the toppings, then pile the roasted garbanzo beans on top. Garnish with an extra pinch of minced mint leaves.

LEMON-HONEYDEW GAZPACHO WITH SPIRULINA OIL

This is the soup I make to impress when I'm entertaining. Between you and me, it's surprisingly simple to make, but the flavors are over the moon in terms of their complex dance, which bounces from sweet to spicy to salty to refreshing. And if all that wasn't enough, this soup is truly fabulous for promoting glowing skin, too. Note that the balance of this recipe depends on the garnish, so don't skip any of the toppings—they are there for more than just show.

MAKES 5 CUPS / 4 SERVINGS

6 cups cubed honeydew melon (peeled and seeded)

¼ cup orange juice, squeezed fresh from 1 orange

1 Tbsp sea buckthorn juice

¼ tsp camu berry powder

¼ tsp ground ancho chile

Pinch cayenne pepper

½ tsp sea salt

½ tsp ground black pepper

2 tsp fresh lemon zest, plus more for serving

2½ Tbsp fresh lemon juice, divided

12 oil-cured black olives, finely minced

2 Tbsp finely minced fennel bulb

1 Tbsp olive oil

¼ tsp spirulina powder

2 Tbsp fennel fronds, for garnish

In a blender, combine the honeydew, orange juice, sea buckthorn juice, camu powder, ancho chile, cayenne, salt, pepper, 2 teaspoons lemon zest, and 2 tablespoons of the lemon juice. Blend until smooth. Transfer to the refrigerator and chill for 30 minutes before serving.

Meanwhile, in a small cup mix together the olives, minced fennel bulb, and remaining ½ tablespoon of lemon juice. Refrigerate the mixture until the soup is ready.

Just before serving, whisk together the olive oil and spirulina powder in a small prep bowl or glass. Stir the soup and then ladle it into chilled bowls. Drizzle with spirulina olive oil. Sprinkle olive-fennel salsa over the bowls and top with additional freshly grated lemon zest and fennel fronds. Even refrigerated, this soup only lasts a short while, so *carpe diem*—make it and enjoy it the same day!

Variation: From a flavor standpoint, you can get away with excluding the sea buckthorn juice, camu powder, and/or spirulina powder... although remember that these are the most powerful, health-giving ingredients in the soup. You can also substitute the honeydew melon with cantaloupe.

AVOCADO PEA SOUP

Kermit was wrong: it is easy being green. This humble, creamy green soup comes together quickly—and is delicious enough to make even a superfood smoothie jealous.

MAKES 6 CUPS / 4 SERVINGS

1 cup mashed avocado

2 cups frozen peas

¼ cup unsweetened coconut-milk yogurt (or plain nondairy yogurt of choice), plus extra for garnish

3½ cups water

4 tsp ume plum vinegar

2 cups baby spinach

½ cup minced mint leaves, plus extra for garnish

1 tsp spirulina powder

Olive oil, for garnish

Ground sumac, for garnish

Purée the avocado, peas, yogurt, water, and ume plum vinegar until creamy. Add the spinach, mint, and spirulina, and blend until smooth. Refrigerate for 30 minutes before serving. Serve chilled, with a splash of extra yogurt, a drizzle of olive oil, a generous sprinkle of sumac, and a few scattered mint leaves.

....

SUPERFOOD BOOST: Add ¼–½ teaspoon camu powder for extra vitamin C, which helps the body absorb all the iron in the spinach more efficiently.

....

WHAT'S UME PLUM VINEGAR?

Ume plum vinegar is made from umeboshi plums, a brined Japanese delicacy that's both salty and sour, and is renowned for enhancing digestion and detoxification. Although this vinegar is sold in many stores, if you can't find it, you can substitute it with red wine vinegar, and add a little extra salt to the recipe to taste.

GOLDENBERRY PEACH GAZPACHO

Bright, loud, and tangy, this soup is a truly tantalizing way to cleanse and excite the palate. I recommend using fresh, super juicy peaches, but if they're not in season, you can get away with using canned peaches (without added sugar, of course).

MAKES 4 CUPS / 4 SERVINGS

4 medium very ripe peaches, peeled, pitted, and chopped (about 3 cups)

⅓ cup dried goldenberries

½ cup yellow bell pepper, chopped

3 Tbsp white wine vinegar

1 Tbsp fresh lemon juice

½ tsp sea salt

¼ tsp ground white pepper, or black pepper

1 Tbsp agave nectar, or liquid sweetener of choice

1 tsp olive oil

1½ cups coconut water

Pinch cayenne pepper

½ cup unsweetened coconut-milk yogurt (or plain nondairy yogurt of choice), for serving

¼ cup chopped pistachios, for garnish

Combine all ingredients except the yogurt and pistachios in a blender. Blend until completely smooth. Taste, and adjust seasoning as desired, then chill the soup for a minimum of 30 minutes before serving. Ladle the soup into small bowls, generously swirl in coconut yogurt on top of the soup, and scatter with pistachios.

SUPERFOOD BOOST: Blend in a small handful of goji berries while puréeing the main soup ingredients for additional antioxidants like lycopene.

CHILLED CARROT-GINGER SOUP

Sweet and smooth with just a wink of spice, this lovely uncooked soup comes together in a flash, proving once again that great recipes don't have to be overly complicated. A little bit of olive oil does wonders to make this soup extra dreamy-creamy. Between the antioxidants in the goji berries and the carrots, this recipe is an exceptional one for eye and skin protection.

MAKES ABOUT 5 CUPS / 4 SERVINGS

4 cups fresh carrot juice

⅓ cup dried goji berries

2 Tbsp pine nuts

½ cup mashed avocado

1 Tbsp grated fresh ginger root

2 Tbsp fresh lime juice

2 Tbsp olive oil (optional)

¼ tsp camu berry powder

¼ tsp cayenne pepper

⅛ tsp sea salt

Combine all the ingredients in a blender and purée until smooth. Chill for a minimum of 30 minutes before serving to allow the flavors to fully meld.

Optional topping: *¼ cup pine nuts, 4 teaspoons dried goji berries, ¼ cup minced tarragon leaves, and ¼ cup unsweetened coconut yogurt. Divide among servings.*

WATERMELON GOJI GAZPACHO

It's hard for me to pick a favorite summer food, but sweetly hydrating watermelon is right up there. It's an ideal accompaniment for long lazy days of bare feet and porch-side living, or on sultry summer evenings, when a melon soup, like this fruity gazpacho, couldn't feel more right. Here, watermelon joins its cooling relative—the cucumber—and sweet goji berries to make a uniquely refreshing soup.

MAKES 5 CUPS / 4 SERVINGS

5 cups chopped watermelon, divided

2 cups peeled and chopped cucumber, divided

¼ tsp ground black pepper

½ cup dried goji berries

¼ cup fresh basil, minced

1 red jalapeño pepper, seeded and minced

¼ cup fresh lime juice

¼ tsp sea salt

Finely dice 1 cup of the watermelon and 1 cup of the cucumber. Transfer to a bowl, add the ground black pepper, and toss to combine. Cover and refrigerate until ready to serve.

Purée all the remaining ingredients in a blender. Chill the soup for a minimum of 30 minutes. To serve, pour into bowls, and top with a mound of cucumber-watermelon salsa.

GREEN JUICE SOUP WITH CUCUMBER NOODLES & RICE *

✳ ◉ ◗ ♥ ⬡

*Though it may sound unusual, this mostly raw, warm-weather soup couldn't be more satisfying...
or healthy. You can make it into a light main meal by including extra tofu and doubling
the portion size, or bring it to work in a mason jar for an enviously healthy lunch.*

MAKES ABOUT 6 CUPS / 4 SERVINGS

1 large cucumber

½ tsp sea salt

2 cups fresh green juice,* chilled

1 Tbsp yellow miso paste

¼ tsp kelp granules

⅛ tsp cayenne pepper

1 cup cooked short brown rice, cooled

1 large avocado, cut into ½-inch dice

½ cup soft tofu, cut into ½-inch dice

¼ cup raw cashews, chopped

2 scallions, white and light green parts, thinly sliced

1 tsp dulse flakes

½ tsp black sesame seeds, for garnish

Fresh cilantro leaves, for garnish

Edible flowers, for garnish (optional)

Trim away the ends of the cucumber. Use a spiralizer to cut the cucumber into spaghetti-like noodles. (Alternatively, use a vegetable peeler to create broader noodles.) Slice long noodles into manageable lengths, about 6 inches. Place noodles in a colander and toss with salt. Set the colander on top of a bowl and drain noodles for 15 minutes. Rinse thoroughly, and then squeeze out any extra liquid to create crunchy, flexible noodles. Refrigerate until ready to use.

In a blender, combine the green juice, miso paste, kelp, and cayenne. Blend until smooth. Taste the mixture: the broth should have a strong but fresh savory flavor. If needed, adjust seasoning: add more miso for a saltier flavor or a little lemon to give it more bite. Add a little water to make the mixture less potent, if you like.

For each serving, place ¼ cup of rice in a shallow bowl. Mound ¼ of the cucumber on top of the rice, and layer with ¼ of the avocado and a little tofu. Pour ½ cup of the green juice broth in the bowl, then scatter the top with chopped cashews, scallions, dulse flakes, black sesame seeds, a couple of cilantro leaves, and flowers (if using). Serve chilled. Refrigerated, Green Juice Soup lasts for up to 2 days.

* For best results, use your favorite unsweetened green juice (homemade or commercial). If you're buying green juice, look for a brand that contains mostly cucumber and celery juice, with additional greens, and very little or no sweet fruit (the sugar content should be under 12 grams per serving). Added ginger and lemon or lime is a definite plus. If green juice is not available, it's easy to make your own—just blend a chopped cucumber with 1 cup of water and strain it through a fine mesh sieve or nut-milk bag. (Or, if available, use a juicer!).

CHILLED TURMERIC COCONUT SOUP

This creamy raw soup delivers layer after layer of flavor—and a bit of umami attitude, too, thanks to a touch of kelp. Be sure to use fresh Thai coconuts (which are easy to find in most supermarkets these days—they're the shaved white ones) and not the hairy (old) variety, which would make this soup far too dense.

MAKES 5 CUPS / 4 SERVINGS

2 young white Thai coconuts

¼ cup fresh orange juice

½ cup orange bell pepper, minced

1 tsp shallot, minced

1 Serrano chile, seeded and minced

½ tsp ground turmeric, plus extra for garnish

1½ tsp kelp granules

2 tsp freshly grated ginger root

1 Tbsp fresh lime juice

½ tsp sea salt

¾ cup ice

Thai basil leaves, for garnish (optional)

Open the coconuts and remove both the coconut water and the interior white flesh. Transfer all the flesh to a blender, and add 2½ cups of the coconut water. Blend until smooth and creamy. Add the orange juice, bell pepper, shallot, Serrano chile, turmeric, kelp, ginger, lime juice, and salt. Blend once more. Stir in the ice and refrigerate for 30 minutes. Blend before serving, and garnish each bowl with a light sprinkle of turmeric powder and a sprig of Thai basil leaves.

SUPERFOOD TIP: If you can't find any young coconuts—no problem. As a substitute, you can blend 1 can of regular canned coconut milk (do not use the reduced-fat variety) with 1 cup of coconut water plus 2 tablespoons of mashed avocado. This will replace the 2 young white coconuts (flesh and water) used in this recipe.

CHILLED WHEATGRASS-ALMOND SOUP WITH FENNEL & GRAPES

This is my superfood take on an ajo blanco, a famous Spanish soup, traditionally made with blanched almonds. It's a glow-inducing recipe, if there ever was one, thanks to the healthy monounsaturated fats that are abundant in almonds. Olive oil helps maintain hydration in the skin, while nutrient-dense powdered sunshine (wheatgrass powder) keeps the body clean and clear from the inside out. Serve this delicate-tasting soup with a farmers market salad for a truly beautiful meal, on every level.

MAKES ABOUT 6 CUPS / 4 SERVINGS

2 large fennel bulbs, with fronds

5 cups water, divided

1 cup raw almonds

¼ cup olive oil, plus extra for serving

1 Tbsp fresh lemon juice

1 tsp apple cider vinegar

¾ tsp sea salt

½ cup ice

2 tsp wheatgrass powder

⅔ cup crisp red seedless grapes, halved

Trim the fennel bulbs, reserving the green stems with the fronds for garnish. Using a mandoline, create about ¼ cup of paper-thin slices from one of the bulbs. Place the slices in an ice water bath, and reserve for garnish. Chop the remaining fennel into dice.

In a small pot, boil 3 cups of water. Place the almonds in a bowl, and pour the boiling water on top. Let the bowl sit for 3–4 minutes, and then drain the water. Squeeze the almonds out of their skins into a bowl.

In a blender, combine the peeled almonds, chopped fennel, olive oil, lemon juice, apple cider vinegar, sea salt, and 2 cups of cold water. Blend until smooth, adding a little extra water if needed (soup should be thick, but able to blend). Add the ice and blend until fully incorporated. Pour 3 cups of the soup into a quart-size mason jar or pitcher. Add the wheatgrass powder to the remaining soup in the blender, and blend to combine. Pour the green mixture into a separate jar or pitcher. Refrigerate both batches for 30 minutes to fully chill.

To serve, alternate pouring in the white and the green soup into each serving bowl once or twice, and run a knife through the surface to draw a decorative swirl. Top with grape halves, a few fennel slices, some plucked fennel fronds, and a few small drops of olive oil for garnish.

EARL GREY ARUGULA SOUP

Earl Grey tea gets its distinct flavor from a combination of black tea and bergamot essence, a fragrance reminiscent of lavender and orange tree blossoms (or in other words, heaven). The flavor of the popular tea complements many types of food, such as fennel, apples, and arugula. This recipe is a great example of the power of using tea instead of broth to create unexpected, alluring flavors, in the healthiest of ways.

MAKES 6 CUPS / 4 SERVINGS

5½ cups water

4 bags Earl Grey tea

2 Tbsp olive oil

½ yellow onion, finely chopped

1 large fennel bulb, finely chopped (about 2 cups)

2 large Fuji apples, cored and finely chopped

1 celery stalk, finely chopped

Sea salt and ground black pepper

3 cups (packed) baby arugula

1 Tbsp coconut sugar

¼ cup raw cashews

2 Tbsp fresh lemon juice

In a medium saucepan, bring the water to a boil. Remove the saucepan from the heat and add the tea bags. Let the mixture steep a minimum of 10 minutes, or until needed for soup.

Warm the oil in a heavy-bottomed pot over medium heat. Add the onion, fennel, apple, celery, ½ teaspoon salt, and a little ground black pepper. Sauté for 6–7 minutes to soften, stirring occasionally.

Discard the tea bags, and add the tea to the vegetables. Bring the mixture to a boil over high heat, cover, and reduce the heat to medium. Cook for 10 minutes. Remove the soup from the heat and stir in the arugula, coconut sugar, cashews, and lemon juice. Working in batches, transfer the soup to a blender, and purée until it is completely smooth. Adjust seasonings if desired. Transfer the soup to a sealable container and refrigerate for a minimum of 2 hours, or until the soup is chilled. Serve cold.

SUPERFOOD BOOST: To get the benefits of more than 70 vitamins and minerals, stir in 1 teaspoon of wheatgrass powder once the soup has cooled.

CHILLED CHOCOLATE (DESSERT) SOUP

Yes, soup for dessert! This silky number is an elegant, delightfully unexpected way to end a meal, and leaves you feeling great thanks to energizing cacao and maca. I recommend using grade B maple syrup in this recipe—it has more flavor than grade A and really brings out the deep notes of the cacao.

MAKES 5 CUPS / 4 SERVINGS

2 medium Hass avocados, peeled and pitted

½ cup cacao powder, plus extra for garnish

2 tsp maca powder

1 tsp vanilla extract

Pinch sea salt

3 cups unsweetened almond milk, plus more as needed

⅓ cup maple syrup (preferably grade B)

1 15-oz can full-fat coconut milk, refrigerated overnight

Combine the avocado, cacao powder, maca powder, vanilla, sea salt, almond milk, and maple syrup in a blender. Purée until smooth. The soup should be creamy and light—if too thick, blend in a little extra almond milk until the desired constancy is reached. Chill in the refrigerator for 1 hour before serving. Refrigerate serving bowls and a small mixing bowl as well.

Just before serving, remove the can of coconut milk from the refrigerator and scoop the white solids into the chilled mixing bowl (discard the remaining water). Whisk the solids into a smooth whip. To serve, pour soup into small chilled serving bowls, and top with a dollop of coconut whip and a light dusting of cacao powder.

Variations: *By adding a shake or two of cinnamon powder and a pinch of cayenne, you can also make a sweet chile-chocolate rendition that's outstanding. Alternately, blend in a little mint extract to make a chocolate-mint version.*

SMOOTH & CREAMY SOUPS

The mere mention of "creamy soup" is enough for most of us to sign up with an enthusiastic "yes!" And just because the soups in this chapter are lusciously smooth doesn't mean they skimp on health benefits, exciting ingredients, or a wide range of flavors. Here you can celebrate cleansing yet rich varieties like the Many Greens Soup (page 107); bask in updated classics, like Potato Leek Soup (page 110); or try something altogether adventurous, like Ginger Yam Bisque with Sea Buckthorn (page 97). Get ready to scrape your soup bowl for every last drop.

✳ = FEATURED SUPERFOOD INGREDIENT

✺ BEAUTY   ◉ BONE STRENGTH   🍃 CLEANSE/DETOX

♥ HEART HEALTH   ☀ IMMUNITY   💧 LOW CALORIE   ⬡ PROTEIN

FRESH CORN SOUP

The not-so-secret key to making a great corn soup is using the cobs for extra flavor: in fact, I almost feel bad for cobless corn soup recipes, which are missing out big-time on their full delicious potential! This soup is delicately complex (you won't taste the energizing boost of reishi at all) and a superb soup to make in the summertime or early fall, when corn is extra crisp and sweet.

MAKES ABOUT 7 CUPS / 4 SERVINGS

6 ears corn, shucked

8 cups water

Sea salt and cracked black pepper

1 Tbsp coconut oil

1 sweet yellow onion (such as Vidalia), diced

Scant ⅛ tsp cayenne pepper

2 tsp reishi powder

2 Tbsp fresh lime juice

2 Tbsp fresh chives, minced

Olive oil, for serving

Cut the kernels from the corncobs, and set them aside in a bowl (you should have about 4½ cups). Place the corncobs in a large saucepan, cover with water, and add ½ teaspoon salt. Simmer over medium heat for 1 hour, or until the liquid is reduced to 2 cups. Discard the cobs, and use a fine mesh sieve to strain the stock over a large bowl. Pour the stock into a holding container, and set aside momentarily (do not refrigerate).

Rinse the saucepan and place it back on the stove. Heat the coconut oil over medium heat, and then add the onion. Cook until translucent, about 3–4 minutes. Add the corn kernels, cayenne, and a big pinch of both salt and pepper. Cook for 12–15 minutes, stirring occasionally, until the corn is tender. Remove the saucepan from the heat and add the stock, reishi powder, and lime juice. Working in batches as needed, ladle the soup into the blender, and purée until very smooth. Taste and adjust seasonings as desired. Ladle the soup into bowls, garnish with chives and a drizzle of olive oil, and serve.

SUPERFOOD TIP: Always use organic corn. Most conventionally grown corn is considered GMO produce.

CREAMED KALE SOUP

Although this creamy soup tastes like the kind that might require loosening your belt buckle (and indeed, it would be worth it), one look at the ingredients makes it clear that this recipe is so healthy it could qualify as a cleanse—thanks to very few calories and an impressive load of micronutrients! Here, puréed cauliflower acts like a rich cream—and adding baby kale at the end of cooking ensures that the soup will retain the maximum amount of vitamins. You can purée the kale completely, or blend it halfway to retain a little bit of texture from the tender leaves.

MAKES 6 CUPS / 4 SERVINGS

2 Tbsp coconut oil

½ white onion, finely chopped

2 stalks celery, finely chopped

2 cloves garlic, minced

4 cups finely chopped cauliflower (florets and stems)

4 cups Miso Broth (page 63, or store bought)

2 Tbsp nutritional yeast flakes

1 Tbsp fresh lemon juice

Dash of your favorite hot sauce (optional)

4 cups (packed) baby kale

Sea salt and ground black pepper

Warm the oil in a heavy-bottomed pot over medium heat. Add the onion, celery, and garlic, and sauté for 3–4 minutes, or until the onion begins to turn a little translucent. Stir in the cauliflower and cook for about 1 minute longer. Pour in the miso broth and increase heat to high. Bring to a boil, cover, and reduce the heat to medium-low. Simmer for about 15 minutes, or until the cauliflower is very soft. Remove from the heat, and stir in the nutritional yeast, lemon juice, and hot sauce (if using). Transfer to a blender and purée until smooth. Add the kale and briefly blend —either leaving in small bits for texture, or blending completely smooth. Season to taste with salt and pepper.

Variation: *To make this a full, balanced meal, stir in 1½ cups protein-rich cooked quinoa or cooked white beans, after blending the kale.*

GINGER-YAM BISQUE WITH SEA BUCKTHORN

The strong flavors of this soup are ideal for serving as a small starter, but if you're so inclined, it's easy to double the quantity for larger servings. If you wish to reduce the amount of sea buckthorn (it's the most expensive ingredient in this recipe), simply add about ½ teaspoon of lime juice to replace each tablespoon of sea buckthorn juice, as lime juice can mimic the berry's sour flavor. (To learn more about sea buckthorn—an amazing superfood—take a look at page 27.)

MAKES 4 CUPS / 4 SERVINGS

2 tsp coconut oil

½ yellow onion, diced

1 large carrot, finely chopped

1 small garlic clove, thinly sliced

1 Tbsp grated fresh ginger root

½ tsp ground turmeric

Pinch cayenne pepper

½ lb yams, peeled and cut into 1-inch dice (about 1¼ cups)

2 cups Vegetable Broth (page 60, or store bought)

½ cup light coconut milk (canned variety)

⅓ cup sea buckthorn juice

½ tsp fresh lime juice

1 Tbsp yacon syrup or maple syrup, plus more for garnish

Sea salt and ground black pepper

Warm the oil in a heavy-bottomed pot over medium heat. Add the onion, carrot, and garlic, and sauté for 5 minutes, stirring occasionally. Stir in the ginger, turmeric, and cayenne, and cook for 1 minute longer. Add the yams and broth, and turn the heat up to high. Bring to a boil, then cover, and reduce the heat to medium-low. Simmer for 15 minutes, until the yams are very soft.

Transfer the mixture to a blender and add the coconut milk, sea buckthorn juice, lime juice, and 1 tablespoon syrup. Purée until completely smooth, then season to taste with salt and pepper. To serve, pour into small serving bowls and drizzle with additional syrup.

SUPERFOOD TIP: Here's a fun idea to get your next party started: give your guests a small, festive cup of a seasonal soup as soon as they walk in the door. What could be more inviting than a warm taste of a healthy soup?

TOMATO-GOJI SOUP WITH FRESH BASIL

Dried goji berries enhance the flavor of tomatoes, with a flirtatious hint of sweetness, offset by the pleasant bite of basil.

MAKES 10 CUPS / 6 SERVINGS

3 lbs tomatoes, preferably heirloom

¼ cup coconut oil

4 large cloves garlic, minced

1½ cups yellow onion, diced

⅔ cup celery, diced

Sea salt and freshly ground black pepper

½ cup dried goji berries

4 cups Vegetable Broth (page 60, or store bought)

⅓ cup (packed) fresh basil, minced, plus additional leaves for garnish

Filtered water

2 Tbsp Hemp Seed Parmesan (page 213), for serving (optional)

Slice the tomatoes in half. Scoop out the seeds and juices and reserve them in a bowl. Cut the tomatoes into dice and set aside. Strain the juicy tomato interior through a fine mesh sieve or two layers of cheesecloth into a bowl, using the back of a spoon or your hands to squeeze out as much liquid as possible—about ⅔ cup. Discard the flesh and seeds, and set the tomato "juice" aside.

Heat the coconut oil in a large saucepan over moderate heat. Add the garlic, onion, celery, and ½ teaspoon sea salt. Cook, stirring often, until the vegetables are softened, about 4–5 minutes. Add the chopped tomatoes and cook for 4–5 minutes longer, or until the tomatoes begin to break down. Add the goji berries and vegetable broth. Bring to a boil, and then reduce the heat to low and simmer for 15 minutes. Remove from the heat and add the reserved tomato juice and basil. Working in batches as needed, transfer soup mixture to a blender. Purée the soup until it is smooth, pouring in water, about ½–1 cup, to thin it to the desired consistency. Taste, and adjust salt and pepper as desired.

Serve the soup warm, topped with a couple of basil leaves and Hemp Seed Parmesan (page 213), as garnish, if desired. Will keep for several days, refrigerated.

SUPERFOOD BOOST: Add ¼ teaspoon dried holy basil, an adaptogenic herb that can boost mood and mental clarity.

ROASTED RED PEPPER SOUP
WITH SEA BUCKTHORN CRÈME FRAÎCHE

Add a protein-rich side salad to this soup, and maybe a slice of toast, and call it dinner.

MAKES 8 CUPS / 4 SERVINGS

4 red bell peppers

⅓ cup raw cashews

4 Tbsp sea buckthorn juice

3 cups + 3 Tbsp water, divided

Smoked salt, or sea salt

2 Tbsp olive oil

1 red onion, diced

1 cup finely chopped fennel (about 1 small bulb)

2 cloves garlic, thinly sliced

2 medium tomatoes, seeded and diced

¼ cup dried goji berries

½ cup white wine

Pinch cayenne pepper

2 Tbsp thinly sliced basil leaves, for serving

Line a baking sheet with foil, and place bell peppers on top. Roast in the oven under a broiler, turning peppers often, until the skin is charred on all sides (about 15–20 minutes). Place the charred peppers in a paper bag, and let the bag sit until the peppers are cool enough to handle.

While the peppers are cooling, make the Sea Buckthorn Crème Fraîche. Combine the cashews, sea buckthorn juice, 3 tablespoons water, and ¼ teaspoon salt in a blender. Blend until completely smooth. Pour into a jar and refrigerate, and leave the blender coated with the remaining crème, for use when it's time to blend the soup.

To prepare the peppers, pull out the cores and seeds, and peel away the charred skins over a large bowl in order to reserve any juices (do not rinse the peppers, or you will wash away some of the flavor). Tear the peppers into large pieces, and set the pepper flesh and juices aside.

Warm the oil in a large saucepan over medium heat. Add the onion, fennel, and garlic and cook for 5 minutes, stirring frequently. Add the roasted bell peppers, tomatoes, goji berries, and white wine. Stir in the cayenne, and ½ teaspoon salt. Continue to cook for 5–6 minutes longer, stirring occasionally, until most of the liquid has evaporated. Add the remaining 3 cups water, and turn the heat to high. Bring the liquid to a simmer, and then remove from the heat. Working in batches as needed, transfer the soup to the blender and purée until completely smooth. Return the soup to the pot and reheat over low. Add salt to taste. To serve, ladle into bowls and drizzle with Sea Buckthorn Crème Fraîche, and scatter a little basil on top.

HARISSA CARROT SOUP

Harissa, the spicy, beloved North African condiment, transforms a perfectly good carrot soup into a truly great one faster than you can grab a bowl. The Goji Harissa isn't too hot in this soup, so if you're craving extra heat (and want to go up a notch on the Scoville scale), add an extra pinch or two of cayenne.

MAKES 6 CUPS / 4 SERVINGS

2 Tbsp olive oil

1 Tbsp caraway seeds

½ yellow onion, diced

1 lb carrots, sliced into ¼-inch-thick rounds

½ lb Yukon gold potatoes, cut into ½-inch dice

1 Tbsp maca powder

5 cups Miso Broth (page 63, or store bought)

½ cup fresh carrot juice

1 tsp apple cider vinegar

1 Tbsp Goji Harissa (page 206), or store-bought red harissa, plus extra for serving

Sea salt and ground black pepper

¼ cup raw cashews, finely chopped

Warm the olive oil in a heavy-bottomed pot over medium heat. Once the oil is hot, add the caraway seeds and cook them until they are fragrant and begin to pop, about 1 minute. Quickly stir in the onion and carrots so as not to burn the caraway, and cook for 10 minutes, to soften, stirring often. Raise the heat to high and stir in the potatoes, maca, and broth. Bring to a boil. Reduce the heat to medium-low to simmer, and cook until the potatoes are soft, about 20–25 minutes.

Transfer the soup to a blender. Add the carrot juice, apple cider vinegar, 1 tablespoon of harissa, and a generous pinch of ground black pepper, and blend until smooth. Return the soup to the pot and gently warm it for 1–2 minutes, and then adjust salt and pepper, if desired. Serve topped with a swirl of harissa to taste, depending on the heat level you desire. Usually about 1 teaspoon of harissa per bowl will do the trick. Garnish the soup with a sprinkle of chopped cashews and serve.

SUPERFOOD BOOST: Add ½ teaspoon ground turmeric to the soup when you add the miso broth.

FENNEL BISQUE
WITH GOLDENBERRY CHUTNEY

To be totally transparent here, you can absolutely get away with making this fennel bisque sans Goldenberry Chutney…and it's still fantastic (just garnish the soup with a couple of fennel fronds from the bulb and call it a day)! But, just as you might sometimes get the urge to dress to impress, the Goldenberry Chutney offers an extra layer of wow (not to mention a nice complement of anti-inflammatory nutrients). Plus, you can make it in no time while you cook the soup…so why not give it a whirl?

MAKES 6 CUPS / 4 SERVINGS

2 Tbsp coconut oil

1 medium yellow onion, sliced thin

2 medium fennel bulbs, trimmed and sliced thin

½ cup dry white wine

1 tsp fennel seeds

4 cups Vegetable Broth (page 60, or store bought)

¼ cup hemp seeds

Sea salt and ground black pepper

½ cup Goldenberry Chutney (page 212), optional

Warm the oil in a heavy-bottomed pot over medium heat. Add the onion and fennel slices and cook for 10 minutes, stirring occasionally, until lightly caramelized. Add the wine and fennel seeds, and cook for 2–3 minutes longer, until the wine has evaporated. Add the vegetable broth and turn heat up to high. Bring to a boil, then reduce the heat to medium-low and cover. Cook for 20 minutes. Stir in the hemp seeds, and then purée the mixture in a blender, working in batches, if needed. Adjust salt and pepper to taste.

If using Goldenberry Chutney, stir ¼ cup into the soup. Ladle into bowls and top with remaining chutney and a sprinkle of black pepper.

SWEET POTATO & MACA SOUP WITH GREEN HARISSA

Unlike some of the extra-powerful superfoods out there, maca is not a flavor that you need to hide. In fact, when it's surround by flavor friends such as roots and tubers, you can use maca almost like you'd use a spice, keeping its flavor in the celebratory foreground. When you taste this immensely exciting soup, which boasts a rich, creamy base highlighted by the abundantly herbaceous taste of Green Harissa, listen closely to the soup and you'll notice a pleasant, slightly sweet, almost butterscotch note—that's the maca!

MAKES 6 CUPS / 4 SERVINGS

½ tsp chili powder

¼ tsp ground cinnamon

¼ tsp ground nutmeg

¼ tsp ground cumin

¼ tsp ground coriander

1 Tbsp coconut oil

1 yellow onion, diced

4 cloves garlic, sliced

1 lb sweet potatoes, peeled and grated

2 Tbsp maca powder

4 cups Vegetable Broth (page 60, or store bought)

¼ cup creamy almond butter

Sea salt and ground black pepper

¼ cup Green Harissa (page 205, or store bought), or more as desired

Chia seeds, for garnish

Cilantro leaves, for garnish

In a small prep bowl, create a spice mix by combining the chili powder, cinnamon, nutmeg, cumin, and coriander, and set aside.

Heat the coconut oil in a heavy-bottomed pot over medium heat. Add the onion and cook until softened, about 7–8 minutes, stirring occasionally. Add the garlic and prepared spice mix, and cook 1 minute longer, stirring constantly. Mix in the sweet potatoes and maca, and then add the vegetable broth and almond butter. Bring the mixture to a boil over high heat, and then reduce the heat to medium-low and simmer for 15 minutes. Transfer the soup to a blender, and purée until smooth. Season to taste with salt and a generous amount of ground black pepper, and add a little water, if needed, to thin the soup. (For a smoother texture, strain the soup through a fine mesh sieve, and reheat gently until ready to serve.) Ladle the soup into serving bowls and swirl a tablespoon of Green Harissa (or more, if you like) on top. Scatter a pinch of chia seeds and cilantro leaves on top as garnish.

MANY GREENS SOUP

Too cold to have a salad? Here's your answer in a cup of cozy soup. You can use any variety of baby greens in this soup—spinach, watercress, baby beet greens, etc. Just be sure not to include lettuces, which don't heat well.

MAKES 6 CUPS / 4 SERVINGS

4 cups Miso Broth (page 63, or store bought)

½ cup raw cashews

1 Tbsp olive oil

2 medium leeks, white and light green parts only, thinly sliced

3 cloves garlic, minced

1 Tbsp fresh thyme, minced

½ lb broccoli, stem peeled and finely chopped, florets chopped small (about 4 cups)

1 cup fresh or frozen peas

6 oz mixed dark baby greens, like spinach, arugula, and kale (about 6 cups, packed)

½ cup (packed) chopped parsley

2 Tbsp fresh lemon juice

Sea salt and ground black pepper

Fresh chives for serving (optional)

Thinly sliced radishes for serving (optional)

In a blender, combine the broth and cashews, and process until smooth. Set aside momentarily.

Warm the oil in a large heavy-bottomed pot over medium heat. Once hot, add the leeks, and sauté for 3–4 minutes, stirring occasionally to soften. Mix in the garlic and cook for 1 minute longer. Add the blended cashew-miso broth, thyme, broccoli, and peas, and bring to a simmer over medium-high heat. Partially cover, leaving the lid slightly ajar, and reduce the heat to medium-low. Cook the mixture for 5 minutes, or until the broccoli is bright green and tender. Uncover and add the baby greens and parsley. Stirring constantly, cook for no more than 1 minute longer, just long enough to wilt the greens. Remove the pot from the heat and transfer the mixture to the blender. Add the lemon juice, ¼ teaspoon sea salt, and ½ teaspoon ground black pepper. Blend until very smooth—this make take a moment. Taste for seasoning and adjust if needed. Ladle into soup bowls and garnish with fresh chives and radish slices, if desired.

FEEL GOOD FACT: From a molecular standpoint, the chlorophyll found in green foods is very similar to hemoglobin, a critical part of our blood that is responsible for transporting oxygen. This explains why chlorophyll-rich vegetables are so effective in replenishing our red blood cells, aiding in increased purification, oxygenation, and energy.

CURRIED APPLE AND BUTTERNUT SQUASH SOUP

Apples and squash go hand-in-hand as BFFs (best flavor friends)…and of course curry makes everything just a little better. This is a wonderfully complex soup you're bound to make time and time again.

MAKES ABOUT 6 CUPS / 4 SERVINGS

1 Tbsp coconut oil

1 yellow onion, diced

1 large sweet apple (such as Fuji), diced (about 1½ cups)

1 Tbsp peeled and minced fresh ginger root

2 lbs butternut squash—peeled, seeded, and cut into 1-inch dice (about 5 cups)

4 cups Miso Broth (page 63, or store bought)

1 Tbsp Thai red curry paste

1 Tbsp dulse flakes

¼ cup dried goji berries

1 tsp ground turmeric

2 Tbsp fresh lime juice

⅔ cup canned coconut milk, plus extra for garnish

Salt and pepper (optional)

½ sweet apple, shaved thin, for garnish

Warm the oil in a large heavy-bottomed pot over medium heat. Add the onion, and cook until translucent, about 5 minutes. Stir in the apple and ginger, and cook 1 minute longer. Add the butternut squash, broth, curry paste, dulse flakes, goji berries, turmeric, and lime juice and mix well. Over high heat, bring to a boil. Reduce the heat to low, cover, and simmer for 30–40 minutes, or until the squash is very soft.

Working in batches, transfer the soup to a blender. Purée until very smooth, and then pour into a large bowl. Repeat with the remaining soup mixture, and return the batches to the soup pot. Stir in ⅔ cup coconut milk and gently warm over low heat for 1–2 minutes. Season with salt and pepper if desired. To serve, ladle into bowls, drizzle with additional coconut milk, and garnish with a few apple shavings.

POTATO LEEK SOUP

This soup is the very definition of creamy, even though it's dairy-free. Hemp seeds and tahini paste do a magnificent job of adding a luscious smoothness to the soup, while adding protein and minerals, like iron and calcium, at the same time.

MAKES 8 CUPS / 6 SERVINGS

2 Tbsp coconut oil

2 leeks, white and light green parts, halved and sliced thin

1 medium white onion, diced

3 cloves garlic, minced

2 bay leaves

Sea salt and ground white (or black) pepper

6 cups Miso Broth (page 63, or use store bought)

1½ lbs russet potatoes (about 2 large), peeled and chopped

¼ cup hemp seeds

1 Tbsp tahini paste

1 tsp chopped fresh thyme

1 Tbsp nutritional yeast

¼ cup minced fresh chives

Warm the oil in a large heavy-bottomed pot over medium heat. Add the leeks, onion, and garlic, and cook for 5 minutes to soften. Reduce the heat to low, add the bay leaves, and stir in ½ teaspoon sea salt. Cover, and cook, stirring occasionally, for 20–25 minutes. Increase the heat to medium-high, add the broth and potatoes, and bring to a boil. Reduce the heat to a simmer, and cook until the potatoes are tender when pierced with a fork, about 10–15 minutes. Remove from the heat and discard the bay leaves. Stir in the hemp seeds, tahini, thyme, and nutritional yeast.

Working in batches as needed, transfer the mixture to a blender, and purée until completely smooth. Taste the soup and season with salt and ground pepper, as desired. Return the soup to the pot in order to keep it warm. To serve, pour the warm soup into individual bowls, and sprinkle generously with chives and ground pepper.

ROASTED BROCCOLI SOUP

There are few vegetables that do not benefit from a brief roast, and broccoli is certainly no exception, which gives this recipe a satisfying smoky taste. Add a jolt of lemon juice, and you have a bright (yet comforting) soup that delivers goodness in both taste and health benefits, like protein and iron.

MAKES 5 CUPS / 4 SERVINGS

- 1 lb broccoli florets, cut into 1-inch pieces (about 3½ cups)
- 2 Tbsp olive oil, divided use, plus more for garnish
- Sea salt and ground black pepper
- 2 cloves garlic, minced
- ¼ tsp red pepper flakes
- 4 cups Miso Broth (page 63, or store bought)
- 3 Tbsp raw cashews
- 2 Tbsp hemp seeds, plus more for garnish
- 1 Tbsp dulse flakes
- 1 Tbsp nutritional yeast
- 2 Tbsp + 1 tsp fresh lemon juice, divided

Preheat the oven to 400°F. On a baking sheet, toss the broccoli florets with 1½ tablespoons olive oil, and season with sea salt and ground black pepper. Roast the broccoli for 20 minutes or until it is tender and slightly blackened. Remove the pan from the oven, set aside five or six medium florets for garnish, and transfer the remaining broccoli to a bowl.

In a heavy-bottomed pot, warm the remaining ½ tablespoon olive oil over medium heat. Add the garlic and red pepper flakes, and cook for 1 minute, stirring constantly. Add the broth and the contents from the bowl of broccoli. Bring to a simmer, and cook for 5 minutes. Transfer the soup to a blender and add the cashews, hemp seeds, dulse flakes, nutritional yeast, and 2 tablespoons of lemon juice. Blend until smooth and creamy. Taste for seasoning and adjust as needed.

When ready to serve, chop the reserved broccoli pieces into very small florets. Mix with the remaining 1 teaspoon lemon juice in a small bowl. Ladle the soup into bowls, and drizzle lightly with a few drops of olive oil, using the back of a spoon to swirl the oil on the surface a couple of times. Top with a cluster of the chopped broccoli, and sprinkle with hemp seeds. Serve warm.

SIX MUSHROOM SOUP

This soup is full of secrets. Secret number 1 is the immense healing power of this soup, thanks to all the mushrooms (see page 18 for all the details about the astonishing health benefits of these special ingredients). Secret number 2 is that this recipe is much more flexible than you might think: if you're missing a mushroom or two of a certain variety, you can easily swap in another, as long as you keep the same total quantity of fresh and powdered mushrooms that is called for in the recipe (technically, you can even make this Two Mushroom Soup, if it's more your style). And secret number 3 is that mushroom soup is quite possibly the best thing ever, needing very little extra ingredient oomph to get its flavorful point across. Don't thank me for the deliciousness of this soup. Thank the mushrooms!

MAKES ABOUT 6 CUPS / 4 SERVINGS

4½ cups Miso Broth (page 63)

¼ cup raw cashews

1 tsp chaga powder

1 tsp reishi powder

1 tsp cordyceps powder

2 Tbsp coconut oil

⅓ cup minced shallot, finely chopped

1 clove garlic, minced

8 oz crimini or portobello mushrooms, chopped

8 oz shiitake mushrooms, chopped

6 oz maitake mushrooms (or use portobello), chopped

1 Tbsp chopped fresh thyme

Sea salt and freshly ground black pepper

Chopped parsley, for garnish

Combine the broth, cashews, and all three mushroom powders in a blender, and process until smooth.

Warm the coconut oil in a heavy-bottomed pot on medium heat. Add the shallot and garlic and cook until softened, about 2 minutes. Add all the chopped mushrooms, thyme, and ¼ cup of the cashew-broth mixture and cook, stirring constantly, until the mushrooms have softened, about 3–4 minutes. Add the remaining cashew-broth mixture, season with ½ teaspoon sea salt and a little ground black pepper, and bring to a boil. Reduce the heat to low and simmer, uncovered, for 20 minutes.

Pour half the soup into a blender, and blend until smooth. Add the remaining soup, and blend for just a moment to incorporate, while leaving in some texture from the chopped mushrooms. Add additional water to thin the soup, if needed, and adjust seasoning if desired. Ladle the soup into bowls and serve with a pinch of freshly chopped parsley.

CELERIAC SOUP
WITH APPLESAUCE & WATERCRESS

If, by chance, you're not already cooking regularly with celeriac—otherwise known as celery root—get ready for a new love affair. This potato-like tuber is so rich in rooty flavor, it needs very little encouragement from seasoning to transform it into the most delightful soup. I like to use a little maca powder to sweeten it slightly, but I add it at the very end of cooking, as maca becomes more pronounced in flavor the longer it is exposed to heat. Peppery fresh watercress and a bit of fruity applesauce contrast nicely with the warming creamy base of this soup.

MAKES 8 CUPS / 6 SERVINGS

1 Tbsp coconut oil

¼ yellow onion, finely chopped

1 stalk celery, finely chopped

1 medium carrot, finely chopped

1 lb celeriac, peeled and cut into ½-inch dice (about 5 cups)

1 large russet potato, peeled and cut into ½-inch dice (about 3 cups)

6 cups Miso Broth (page 63, or store bought)

Sea salt and ground black pepper

1 tsp apple cider vinegar

1 Tbsp maca powder

2 Tbsp hemp seeds

½ cup unsweetened applesauce, for serving

1½ cups watercress, for serving

Heat the oil in a large heavy-bottomed pot over medium heat. Add the onion, celery, and carrot, and stir often until softened, about 8–10 minutes. Add the celeriac, potato, broth, ¼ teaspoon of sea salt, and a bit of freshly ground black pepper. Over high heat, bring the mixture to a boil. Cover, and reduce the heat to low. Simmer for 30 minutes, or until the celeriac and potato are very soft. Remove from the heat and stir in the apple cider vinegar, maca, and hemp seeds. Working in batches, transfer the soup to a blender and purée until smooth. If needed, rewarm the blended soup on the stove and season with additional salt and pepper, if desired. To serve, ladle into bowls and top soup with a generous swirl of applesauce, a nest of watercress, and a sprinkle of ground black pepper.

PURÉED TURNIP SOUP

When I first made this soup many years ago, I was so enamored of it I wrote a tribute post on my website titled "Turnips: The Forgotten Tuber." Since then, I've elevated the recipe further, adding both maca and yacon, which enhance the flavor of the soup, as well as its energizing qualities. Perhaps now the title of my original tribute should be updated, and more accurately renamed "Turnips, Maca, and Yacon: The Complete Forgotten Tuber Collection."

MAKES 6 CUPS / 4 SERVINGS

2 Tbsp coconut oil

1 medium yellow onion, chopped

2 large cloves garlic, minced

1 lb turnips, diced into ½-inch pieces (3 cups)

1 lb sweet potatoes, peeled and diced into ½-inch pieces (2 cups)

2½ cups Vegetable Broth (page 60, or store bought)

1 cup unsweetened almond milk

1 Tbsp maca powder

¼ cup dried yacon slices, plus additional for garnish

Sea salt and ground black pepper

Warm the oil in a heavy-bottomed pot over medium heat. Add the onion and garlic and sauté for 5 minutes, stirring occasionally. Add the turnips and sweet potatoes, then pour in the broth and almond milk. Stir in the maca, yacon, ¼ teaspoon sea salt, and ½ teaspoon ground black pepper. Turn the heat up to high and bring to a boil. Cover, reduce the heat to medium-low, and simmer for 15–20 minutes, or until the turnips and sweet potatoes are tender.

Transfer the mixture to a blender, and purée until it is completely smooth (blend in a couple of small batches, if necessary). Adjust seasonings as desired. Pour the soup into bowls, and top with a sprinkle of black pepper and a few slices of yacon.

SUPERFOOD BOOST: Before serving the soup, swirl a little Green Harissa (page 205) or Goji Harissa (page 206) on top.

TRUFFLED ASPARAGUS SOUP

Divinely musky truffle oil gives the illusion of grandeur to a dish—it's a pantry investment that will take your soups from good to fabulous. Combined with a bit of briny dulse, truffle oil helps bring out incredible flavor from the oft-subdued asparagus.

MAKES 6 CUPS / 4 SERVINGS

1 lb fresh asparagus

4 medium leeks, white parts halved and sliced thin, green parts halved and reserved*

6 cups water

Sea salt and ground black pepper

2 Tbsp olive oil

3 large cloves garlic, minced

2 tsp dulse flakes, plus more for serving

¼ cup hemp seeds

2 Tbsp fresh lime juice

1/16 tsp cayenne pepper

1 Tbsp white truffle oil, plus more for serving

*Be sure to wash the halved leeks very well, especially the greens, as they can be sandy.

Trim the pointed asparagus tips from the stem, about 1 inch in length, and reserve. Snap off the woody stems from each spear and reserve. Cut the remaining stem in ½-inch pieces and set aside.

Add the green parts of the leeks and the woody asparagus stems to a medium pot, and add the water and ½ teaspoon sea salt. Bring to a boil, then reduce the heat to low, cover, and simmer for 20 minutes. With a slotted spoon, remove and discard the leeks and asparagus. While the stock is still boiling, add the asparagus tips, and blanch for 1–2 minutes until the tips turn bright green. Turn off the heat, remove the tips with a slotted spoon, and set them aside to use as a garnish. Pour the stock into a bowl to reserve.

Rinse the pot, then return it to the stove and warm the olive oil over medium heat. Add the garlic and sliced leeks, and cook until softened, about 3–4 minutes. Add the sliced raw asparagus stems, reduce the heat to low, cover, and cook for 10 minutes or until tender, stirring occasionally. Add the dulse flakes and the reserved stock. Bring to a boil, reduce the heat to a simmer, and cook for 15 minutes, covered. Transfer the soup to a blender, working in batches if necessary. Add the hemp seeds, lime juice, cayenne, ¼ teaspoon ground black pepper, and 1 tablespoon truffle oil. Blend until completely smooth. Taste and adjust the salt as desired, and add additional water if the soup needs thinning. Serve the soup with asparagus tips bundled on top, a very light drizzle of truffle oil, and a sprinkle of dulse flakes and freshly ground black pepper.

CUMIN BEET SOUP

Look at that color: is there anything more show-stopping than a creamy beet soup? Here, maca (another superfood root) lends an additional layer of sweet, earthy flavor, while a pinch of cumin and chili powder take this beautiful soup to an even higher level of delicious. Though it may be tempting to use reduced-fat canned coconut milk, I don't recommend using it here: your soup will be much more balanced with a full-fat selection.

MAKES 6 CUPS / 4 SERVINGS

1 lb beets (about 3–4 medium), trimmed and scrubbed

1 Tbsp coconut oil

½ tsp cumin seeds

2 cloves garlic, minced

1 large yellow onion, diced

1 Tbsp maca powder

½ tsp ground turmeric

¼ tsp chili powder

½ tsp sea salt

2 cups water

1 13.5 oz can coconut milk, divided

2 tsp dulse flakes

1 Tbsp fresh lemon juice

Ground sumac, for garnish (optional)

Beet sprouts, for garnish (optional)

Preheat the oven to 375°F. Wrap the beets individually in aluminum foil, and place them on a baking sheet. Roast the beets for 60–90 minutes, or until they're very soft. Remove the beets from the oven and let them sit until they are cool enough to handle. Peel away and discard the beet skins, and chop the beets into dice. Set aside.

Warm the coconut oil in a medium saucepan over medium heat. Add the cumin seeds and lightly toast until fragrant, about 1 minute. Add the garlic and onion and cook, stirring occasionally, until softened, about 3–4 minutes. Add the maca, turmeric, chili powder, salt, and water. Bring to a boil, and then reduce the heat to low and simmer for 15 minutes. Stir in 1½ cups coconut milk and simmer for 1 minute to warm. Transfer the soup to a blender, and add the dulse flakes and lemon juice. Purée until smooth—be sure to blend very thoroughly for an evenly silky texture. Serve warm, drizzled with remaining coconut milk, a sprinkle of sumac, and beet sprouts for garnish.

CREAMY ZUCCHINI SOUP

Zucchini is pleasurably deceptive. Who would have thought that it could be transformed, with just a little puréeing, from a watery, bland vegetable into a creamy, satisfying soup? Here, its subtle flavor is enhanced by a note of umami from kelp, and a bright perk from basil. For a simpler variation, swap out the suggested garnishes with a swipe of tapenade.

MAKES ABOUT 9 CUPS / 6 SERVINGS

2 Tbsp olive oil, plus more for garnish

2 large cloves garlic, minced

1 large yellow onion, diced

½ tsp fresh thyme leaves

1 bay leaf

3 lbs zucchini, trimmed and sliced thin

2 tsp kelp granules

4 cups Vegetable Broth (page 60, or store bought)

Sea salt and ground black pepper

¼ cup fresh basil leaves, sliced thin, plus additional for garnish

¼ cup hemp seeds, plus additional for garnish

In a large saucepan, warm the olive oil over medium heat. Add the garlic, onion, and thyme leaves. Cook, stirring occasionally, until softened, about 5 minutes. Add the bay leaf, zucchini, kelp, broth, ½ teaspoon sea salt, and ½ teaspoon ground black pepper. Increase the heat to bring to a boil, and then reduce the heat to a low simmer for 10 minutes, or until the zucchini is tender. Remove from the heat, discard the bay leaf, and add the basil and hemp seeds. Working in batches, transfer to a blender, and purée until smooth. Return the blended soup to the stovetop and keep warm on lowest heat until ready to serve—adjust seasonings as desired. Serve warm, drizzled lightly with olive oil, and sprinkled with hemp seeds and freshly ground black pepper. Scatter a few basil leaves over the top.

FEEL GOOD FACT: Kelp is exceptionally high in iodine—far more than any other seaweed (with almost 3 times as much as dulse). This quality makes kelp exceptionally valuable for thyroid health and weight management. Though it is often sold as a supplement to boost metabolism, why not directly enhance the foods you eat with kelp's beneficial salty flair?

PARSNIP-PEAR SOUP

When I originally developed this soup for a Thanksgiving feature in Vegetarian Times, *little did I know it would become such an integral part of my cooking repertoire at home! My family adores this slightly sweet soup, which has enjoyed a few superfood tweaks through the years, as so many great recipes do. For this soup, use the softest, ripest pears you can find, taking advantage of the natural sugars the fruit develops as it matures.*

MAKES 10 CUPS / 6 SERVINGS

1 Tbsp coconut oil

2 leeks, white and light green parts only, cleaned and sliced thin

1½ lbs parsnips, peeled and cut into ½-inch rounds

2 very soft pears, any variety, cored and diced

¼ tsp ground nutmeg

⅛ tsp cayenne pepper

2 Tbsp dried goji berries

4 cups Vegetable Broth (page 60, or store bought)

3 cups water

2 Tbsp almond butter

2 Tbsp hemp seeds

1 Tbsp yacon syrup or maple syrup, plus more for garnish

2 Tbsp flat parsley leaves

Sea salt and ground black pepper

In a large stockpot, warm the coconut oil over medium heat. Add the leeks and sauté for 4 minutes. Add the parsnips, pears, nutmeg, and cayenne, and cook for 2 minutes longer, stirring often. Add the goji berries, and pour in the broth and water, and season with a big pinch of salt and a generous amount of black pepper. Turn up the heat and bring to a boil. Lower heat to medium-low, partially cover the pot, and simmer for 25 minutes or until the parsnips are tender. Remove from heat and stir in the almond butter, hemp seeds, and syrup.

Transfer the soup to a blender, in batches as needed, and blend until smooth. Return the soup to the stock pot—adjust seasonings and add extra water, if needed, to thin soup.

To serve, ladle the soup into bowls. Garnish with fresh parsley, ground black pepper, and a drizzle of yacon or maple syrup.

GOLDEN CAULIFLOWER SOUP WITH SEARED MUSHROOMS

Both the cauliflower and the turmeric in this soup are well-studied anti-cancer and anti-inflammatory ingredients, helping you glow from within with health.

MAKES 6 CUPS / 4 SERVINGS

2 Tbsp shelled raw pistachios

¼ tsp wheatgrass powder (optional)

Sea salt

1 Tbsp coconut oil

2 leeks, white and light green parts only, sliced thin

2 cloves garlic, minced

1½ lbs cauliflower, cut into 1-inch pieces (4 cups)

1 tsp fresh thyme leaves, minced

½ tsp ground turmeric

¼ tsp cayenne pepper

4 cups Miso Broth (page 63)

½ cup raw cashews

1 cup wild mushrooms, such as maitake, shiitake, and/or chanterelle

1 Tbsp grapeseed oil

2 Tbsp minced fresh parsley

¼ cup microgreens and edible flowers, for garnish (optional)

Chop the pistachios very finely into a coarse powder. Place the powder in a small bowl and add the wheatgrass powder as well as a scant ¼ teaspoon sea salt. Set aside.

Warm the coconut oil in a heavy-bottomed pot over medium heat. Add the leeks and garlic, and cook for 2–3 minutes until leeks are softened. Stir in the cauliflower and thyme, and cook for a minute longer. Add the turmeric, cayenne, and miso broth, and turn the heat up to high. Bring to a boil, cover, and reduce heat to medium low. Cook for 20 minutes, or until cauliflower is very soft. Remove the pot from the heat, and add the cashews. Transfer the soup to a blender, working in batches as needed, and purée until completely smooth. Return the soup to the pot and keep warm.

Depending on the size and variety of mushrooms you use, tear into bite-size portions, or slice into ¼-inch pieces. Warm the grapeseed oil in a large skillet over high heat. Once the oil is shimmering, add the mushrooms, spreading out in an even layer as much as possible. Without stirring, cook the mushrooms for 1–2 minutes to sear. When the mushroom bottoms have turned golden, flip them over with a spatula and repeat on the other side for 1–2 minutes longer. Transfer the mushrooms to a bowl, add the parsley, season with salt, and toss well.

Serve the soup by ladling it into bowls and sprinkling with ground pistachios. Place a mound of mushrooms on top, and dress up the plate with microgreens and flowers as desired.

SMOKY PUMPKIN SOUP WITH CANDIED SEED CLUSTERS

One magical October, I spent a week in Salem, Massachusetts, when autumn was at its prime and the town was bursting with seasonal spirit. The last night I was there, I ordered a bowl of fabulous smoked pumpkin soup at a small café that I would never forget. I make my own version every year now, starting as soon as the weather turns crisp.

MAKES 8 CUPS / 4–6 SERVINGS

1 medium sugar pumpkin, about 3½ lbs

3 Tbsp coconut oil, divided

Sea salt and ground black pepper

2 sprigs fresh rosemary

2 small leeks, white and light green parts only, sliced thin

4 cups Vegetable Broth (page 60, or store bought)

½ cup fresh orange juice

2 large Medjool dates, pitted

⅓ cup dried goji berries

2 tsp chaga powder

½ tsp hickory liquid smoke

¼ tsp ground allspice

¼ cup Candied Seed Clusters (page 211)

Preheat the oven to 375°F.

Cut the stem off of the pumpkin and discard. Place the pumpkin cut side down, and slice in half. Scrape out all of the seeds and stringy fiber. Rub the inside of each half with ½ tablespoon of coconut oil, season with salt and pepper, and tuck a sprig of rosemary inside. Place the halves facedown on a baking sheet or roasting pan, and add a few tablespoons of water to the pan. Roast for 60–90 minutes, or until the pumpkin is very soft and a fork slides easily through the flesh. Remove from the oven. When cool enough to handle, use a spoon to scoop the flesh away from the skin. Discard the skin as well as the rosemary stem.

In a heavy-bottomed pot, warm the remaining 2 tablespoons coconut oil over medium heat. Add the leeks, and cook until softened, about 3–4 minutes. Add the pumpkin, broth, orange juice, dates, goji berries, chaga, liquid smoke, and allspice, and bring to a boil. Reduce the heat to medium-low and simmer for 10 minutes. Working in batches, transfer the soup to a blender and purée. Return the soup to the pot, season to taste with salt and pepper, and keep warm. Serve with Candied Seed Clusters scattered on top.

Variation: *Low on time? Use two 15-ounce cans of pumpkin purée instead of roasting the pumpkin.*

CACAO CHESTNUT SOUP

The mere mention of chestnuts immediately transports me to the bustling streets of New York City in the winter. Central Park is lined with food stands, where the aroma of warm, freshly roasted chestnuts wafts cheerily, daring anyone to stop and not buy a bag—even a small one (I have never been able to resist this—not once). When I'm back at home in California, making a pot of chestnut soup perfectly encapsulates the mood—well, almost. This soup is a beautiful play between rich and light—like satin sheets for your tongue—and cacao and maca enhance the earthy-sweet nuttiness of this savory (yes, savory cacao!) soup even further, giving it a unique superfood spin. **Note:** *If you're not up for using brandy, just use extra vegetable broth in its place.*

MAKES 5 CUPS / 4 SERVINGS

2 Tbsp coconut oil

½ small red onion, finely chopped

1 carrot, finely chopped

1 celery stalk, finely chopped

10 oz roasted chestnuts (about 2 vacuum-packed bags or 1 jar)

1 bay leaf

¼ cup brandy

4 cups Vegetable Broth (page 60, or store bought)

2 Tbsp cacao powder, plus extra for garnish

1 Tbsp maca powder

½ cup raw cashews

¼ tsp ground nutmeg

⅔ cup water, plus more as needed

Sea salt and ground black pepper

Warm the coconut oil in a heavy-bottomed pot over medium heat. Add the onion, carrot, and celery, and sauté until very soft, about 8–10 minutes, seasoning lightly with salt and pepper. Add the chestnuts, bay leaf, and brandy. Cook, stirring, until the brandy has mostly evaporated, about 2–3 minutes. Add the broth and stir in the cacao powder and maca powder. Turn heat up to high and bring to a boil. Reduce the heat to medium-low, and gently simmer, uncovered, for 20 minutes.

While the soup is simmering, combine the cashews, nutmeg, water, and ¼ teaspoon sea salt in a blender. Blend until smooth and creamy. Pour ⅓ cup of the mixture into a jar or glass, and reserve for serving; leave the remaining cream in the blender.

When the soup has finished cooking, discard the bay leaf, and transfer the soup to the blender (which should still contain some of the cream). Purée the mixture until smooth. Add a little additional water to thin the soup if needed, and season to taste. To serve, pour the soup into small serving bowls and swirl some cashew cream on top. Dust the soup lightly with additional cacao powder and serve warm.

PERSIMMON HOLIDAY SOUP

Persimmons are some of the most cheerful fruits on the planet and always remind me of early fall, when they hang off the bare trees like jolly orange ornaments. They also do a wonderful job of lending creamy sweetness to a soup like this one. **A tip:** *If you're using Hachiya persimmons, they should be extremely soft (and feel like a water balloon), otherwise they will taste too puckery. On the other hand, Fuyu persimmons should be hard and crisp.*

MAKES 12 CUPS / 8 SERVINGS

2 Tbsp coconut oil

½ red onion, finely chopped

2 lbs parsnips, peeled and cut into ½-inch dice

1½ lbs very soft Hachiya persimmons, trimmed and chopped

2 Tbsp dried goji berries

2 tsp maca powder

1 cinnamon stick

6 cups Vegetable Broth (page 60, or store bought)

2 cups (unsweetened) vanilla almond milk

Sea salt and ground black pepper

1 Fuyu persimmon, shaved into paper-thin slices, for garnish (optional)

1 cup fresh pomegranate seeds

½ cup roasted hazelnuts, chopped

Warm the oil in a heavy-bottomed pot over medium heat. Add the onion and parsnips and sauté for 6–7 minutes, or until the parsnips begin to turn golden. Add the Hachiya persimmons, goji berries, maca powder, cinnamon stick, and broth. Raise the heat to high, and bring the mixture to a boil; then reduce the heat to medium-low, cover, and cook for 20 minutes. Remove the mixture from the heat and stir in the almond milk and a little ground black pepper. Discard the cinnamon stick. Working in batches, purée the soup in a blender. Return the soup to the pot over low heat to keep it warm. If the soup is too thick, add a little water. Taste for salt and adjust as desired.

To serve, ladle the soup into bowls and garnish with a couple of persimmon slices, pomegranate seeds, chopped hazelnuts, and a sprinkle of ground black pepper.

ROASTING HAZELNUTS: Place the hazelnuts in a small sauté pan over medium heat for 5–10 minutes, stirring frequently to keep them from burning. The hazelnuts will be ready when they are slightly browned and fragrant. Let them cool, and then chop them into small bits. Alternatively, if you happen to have a fire going, place the hazelnuts in a fire-safe pan and hold it over the flames for 2–4 minutes, shaking the pan to avoid burning.

BROTHY & NOODLE SOUPS

Is it any wonder that brothy noodle soups are considered a classic go-to remedy for healing and rejuvenation? These beauties combine a kaleidoscopic array of natural whole foods set afloat in decidedly aromatic broths—delightful riffs on texture and flavor that make it tempting to ask for another serving (or two). Whether you choose a vegetable-centric recipe like Springtime Minestrone (page 151) or a noodle-packed bowl of Miso Noodle Soup (page 139), rest assured, every spoonful has a lot to offer.

✳ = FEATURED SUPERFOOD INGREDIENT

✳ BEAUTY   ☯ BONE STRENGTH   🌿 CLEANSE/DETOX

♥ HEART HEALTH   ☀ IMMUNITY   💧 LOW CALORIE   ⬡ PROTEIN

SHAVED BRUSSELS SPROUTS SOUP WITH COCONUT BACON BITS

This soup exudes a certain brash confidence—like showing up to a party in a pair of old jeans and T-shirt, because you're good enough just as you are, thank you very much. Whip up the Cashew Sour Cream and Coconut Bacon while the soup is simmering, and you'll have a hearty bowl to enjoy in less than half an hour. While I like to keep some texture in this soup, you can also purée it if it's more your style. Either way, it's lovely served with a thick slice of rustic bread.

MAKES 10 CUPS / 6 SERVINGS

1½ lbs Brussels sprouts

3 Tbsp coconut oil

2 leeks, white and light green parts sliced thin

2 medium potatoes, peeled and cut into ½-inch cubes

2 tsp fresh thyme leaves

8 cups Vegetable Broth (page 60, or store bought)

Sea salt and ground black pepper

¾ cup Cashew Sour Cream (page 210, or store bought), divided

½ cup Coconut Bacon Bits (page 209)

Use a mandoline to thinly shave the Brussels sprouts, or slice as thinly as possible with a knife.

Warm the oil in a heavy-bottomed pot over medium heat. Add the leeks and potatoes and cook 2 minutes, stirring. Add the shaved Brussels sprouts and thyme, and cook for 1 minute longer. Pour in the broth—if you are using a salted broth, wait to season until the end of cooking; if you're using unsalted (or low-salt) broth, add a couple of pinches of salt. Turn heat up to high and bring to a boil, then cover the pot and reduce the heat to medium-low. Simmer for 15–20 minutes, or until the potatoes are very soft. Remove from the heat, and stir in 4 tablespoons Cashew Sour Cream. Season to taste with salt and pepper. Serve topped with remaining Cashew Sour Cream and Coconut Bacon Bits.

SUPERFOOD BOOST: To give the soup even more immune-boosting power, add 2 tablespoons of your favorite medicinal mushroom powder after adding the broth. A half cup of hemp seeds can also be added for a protein-rich garnish.

GOJI-SAFFRON SOUP WITH SORGHUM

I love the slightly sweet-sour flavor of goji berries combined with floral saffron and chewy, protein-rich sorghum in this brothy soup.

MAKES 7 CUPS / 4 SERVINGS

- 6 cups Vegetable Broth (page 60, or low-sodium store-bought variety), divided
- 1 pinch saffron
- 2 Tbsp olive oil
- 1 medium yellow onion, finely diced
- 1 medium fennel bulb, finely diced
- 3 cloves garlic, minced
- 2 bay leaves
- ½ cup dried goji berries
- 1 cup cooked sorghum (see box below)
- 1 cup dry white wine
- ½ tsp sea salt, or to taste
- 2 Tbsp minced fresh parsley, divided use

In a small pot, bring 1 cup of the vegetable broth to a simmer. Remove from the heat. Finely crumble the saffron threads by hand (or grind them in a mortar and pestle—the finer they're ground, the better the flavor), and stir them into the broth. Let the broth sit while you continue to make the soup.

In a separate heavy-bottomed large pot, warm the oil over medium heat. Add the onion and fennel, and cook for 5 minutes, stirring occasionally. Mix in the garlic, and cook for a couple of minutes longer to allow the vegetables to lightly caramelize. Stir in the bay leaves, goji berries, and cooked sorghum, and then add the wine, saffron broth, remaining vegetable broth, and ½ teaspoon sea salt. Bring to a boil over high heat, then reduce the heat to medium-low, cover, and cook for 30 minutes. Discard the bay leaves, stir in 1 tablespoon of the parsley, and adjust the salt to taste. Ladle the soup into bowls, and sprinkle the remaining parsley on top.

....

COOKING SORGHUM: Place 1 cup dry sorghum in a medium pot and cover with water, 2 inches above the grain. Bring the water to a boil and then reduce the heat to a simmer and cook for 45–75 minutes (time will vary depending on the freshness of the grain, but it usually takes about 1 hour). The grain is cooked through when it is soft but still has a bit of a chew (the consistency is similar to wild rice). Drain off any excess water. **1 cup dry sorghum = 2 cups cooked sorghum**

....

CHIA TORTILLA SOUP WITH BLACK BEANS

There are enough tortilla soup recipes in the world to fill this book and probably a dozen more, but it's a favorite for good reason. My homestyle recipe for tortilla soup comes close to the authentic, simple version, but also touts the health benefits of chia, Mexican superfood extraordinaire, as well as hearty black beans. To make this recipe extra nutrient-dense, I always use baked tortillas instead of deep-fried—the difference in flavor is negligible and you'll avoid one of the unhealthiest cooking practices with delicious results. I like to double the recipe when I make this soup for friends, because there's always someone asking for seconds (and the recipe)!

MAKES 4 SERVINGS

1 dried pasilla or ancho chile

3 vine-ripened tomatoes (about ¾ lb)

¼ white onion, halved, peeled, and trimmed

1 clove garlic, unpeeled

1 Tbsp olive oil

4 cups Vegetable Broth (page 60, or low-sodium store-bought variety)

1½ cups cooked black beans (page 13, or 1 15-oz can, drained)

Sea salt

2 Tbsp chia seeds, for topping

1 cup crushed baked tortilla chips (homemade [page 202] or store bought), for topping

2 cups finely shredded green cabbage, for topping

1 large avocado, sliced, for topping

¼ cup Cashew Sour Cream (page 210, or store bought), for topping

1 lime, quartered, for garnish

Warm a large skillet over medium-high heat. Dry roast the whole dried chile by pressing it firmly onto the hot surface of the pan with a metal spatula for several minutes on each side—the chile should become blackened and slightly puffed. Remove the whole chile from the pan so that it will cool. In the same pan, dry roast the tomatoes, onion, and garlic for 10 minutes, rotating them with a pair of tongs every few minutes, until the vegetables are charred and the tomatoes have begun to soften. Pull the garlic out early, once the skin begins to brown, and remove the peel. Add the charred tomatoes, onion, and peeled garlic to a blender. Open the chile and discard the stem and seeds, and then add it to the blender as well. Purée the mixture until it is smooth.

Heat the oil over medium heat in a heavy-bottomed pot. Add the puréed vegetables and cook until the color deepens, about 5 minutes. Add the vegetable broth and increase the heat to high. Bring to a boil, then reduce the heat to medium-low and simmer for 30 minutes. Add the cooked black beans, and simmer for 10 minutes longer. Remove from the heat and adjust salt to taste. Serve the soup hot, with chia seeds scattered over the top and piled high with tortilla chips, shredded cabbage, avocado, and Cashew Sour Cream. Include lime wedges on the side for a fresh squeeze at the table.

CARAWAY CABBAGE SOUP WITH FREEKEH BALLS

The freekeh balls in this recipe quickly elevate a humble cabbage soup to new heights of savory glory. You'll find the recipe makes more than you'll need for the soup, but as leftovers, they make a delectable protein-rich snack.

MAKES 4 SERVINGS

1 large baking potato, peeled and cut into ½-inch dice, divided

1 cup freekeh

Cooking oil spray

2 Tbsp olive oil, divided use

1 large yellow onion, very finely chopped, divided

4 cloves minced garlic

1 tsp minced fresh rosemary

3 oz shiitake mushrooms, chopped (about 2 cups)

1 Tbsp red wine vinegar

2 Tbsp ground chia seed powder*

2 Tbsp yellow miso paste

¾ cup raw walnuts, chopped

¼ cup hemp seeds

1 large carrot, thinly sliced into half moons

1 stalk celery, thinly sliced

2 tsp caraway seeds, freshly ground

½ medium green cabbage, halved again and thinly sliced

6 cups Vegetable Broth (page 60, or store bought)

Sea salt and ground black pepper

Minced parsley, for serving

Cook the potato and freekeh at the same time. Fill a small pot with water and a big pinch of salt, and bring to a boil over medium-high heat. Fill a second pot with 2½ cups of water and a big pinch of salt, and bring to a boil over high heat. Add ¾ cup of the diced potato to the first pot and simmer until tender, about 10–15 minutes, and drain. Meanwhile, to the second pot, add the freekeh, reduce the heat to medium-low, and cover. Cook the freekeh until all the water has evaporated, about 20 minutes, then remove the pot from the heat and keep covered for 5 minutes to steam.

Preheat the oven to 375°F. Line two baking sheets with parchment and spray with cooking oil.

Warm 1 tablespoon of the oil in a heavy-bottomed pot over medium heat. Add ½ cup of the onion, along with the garlic, and sauté for about 3 minutes to soften, stirring often. Add the rosemary, mushrooms, and vinegar, and cook for about 3 minutes longer, stirring constantly. Transfer the mushroom mixture to a food processor, and add the cooked potatoes, chia seed powder, and miso paste. Purée for a moment until the mixture is fairly smooth. Add the cooked freekeh, walnuts, and hemp seeds, and pulse until just incorporated, while leaving plenty of texture (the mixture will be very soft). Drop the mixture onto the baking sheets in rounded tablespoons, using your fingers to shape the mixture into balls (about 36 total). Bake on the center racks of the oven, flipping the balls with a spatula and rotating the pans halfway

through cooking, until the balls are golden brown on both sides, about 30–35 minutes. Turn off the oven, and leave the balls inside to keep warm and further solidify while you make the soup.

In the same heavy–bottomed pot, warm the remaining 1 tablespoon of oil over medium heat. Add all the remaining onions, as well as the carrot and celery. Sauté the mixture for 5 minutes, stirring it occasionally. Add the caraway, all of the remaining uncooked potato, and the cabbage, and sauté for about 5 minutes longer, or until the cabbage has wilted. Pour in the broth, and bring to a boil over high heat. Cover, reduce the heat to medium-low, and simmer for 20 minutes. Remove from the heat and let soup stand for 5–10 minutes, and then adjust seasonings if desired. Serve by placing several freekeh balls in a shallow soup bowl, then surrounding them with a lake of cabbage soup and broth. Sprinkle with parsley.

* Chia powder can be purchased at the store or made at home by briefly blitzing chia seeds in a spice grinder.

FORBIDDEN GREEN TEA SOUP

For the longest time, I naïvely thought this green tea and rice go-to lunchtime recipe was all mine—a random stroke of brilliance. (Hint: not even close!) After seeing something similar on a menu one day, I immediately launched an in-depth search online. I quickly discovered that this dish is called ochazuke, which means "green tea over rice," in Japanese, and has been enjoyed for centuries. My version is definitely simpler than many of the more traditional recipes, but it does the trick (deliciously) all the same. If you make the rice ahead of time, you can put this soup together in less than 10 minutes.

MAKES 4 SERVINGS

2 cups black forbidden rice

7½ cups filtered water, divided

4 bags genmaicha (toasted rice green tea), or regular green tea

1 Tbsp ume plum vinegar

4 sheets nori, finely crushed

½ cup extra-firm tofu, cut into ¼-inch dice

4 green onions, white and light green parts, thinly sliced

1 medium avocado, diced

To cook the rice, combine the rice and 3½ cups of the water in a saucepan. Bring to a boil, cover, and reduce the heat to a low simmer. Cook the rice for about 30 minutes, and then remove it from the heat. With the cover on, let the rice rest for a few minutes, and then fluff with a fork.

A few minutes before the rice is finished cooking, bring the remaining 4 cups of water to a boil in a medium pot, and then remove it from the heat. Add the tea bags, cover the pot, and let the tea steep for 5 minutes. Squeeze the bags before removing them from the pot to extract the most amount of flavor, and then stir in the ume vinegar. Keep the mixture warm.

Divide the rice among the serving bowls, and then top each with nori, tofu, and green onions. Pour the green tea on top, and add the avocado last. Serve immediately.

Note: *You can make this entire recipe ahead of time, store it in sealable jars, and simply reheat gently when you're ready to serve—just leave out the avocado and add it as a last-minute garnish. This soup may also be served as a cold soup.*

FEEL GOOD FACT: Forbidden rice sounds like something out of a fairy tale—a very dark one! And, as you might expect, there's a bit of history to it: during the Ching and Ming dynasties in China, consuming black rice was the exclusive privilege of the emperor, which was eaten as a means of ensuring health and longevity. Actually, the emperors were on to a good thing, even if you and I would have been forbidden from enjoying it! The antioxidant content in black rice is impressive, including the same heart-healthy anthocyanins that make acai and blueberries such valued foods. And aside from being the highest source of antioxidants of any rice variety, at 5 grams of protein per cooked half-cup serving, forbidden rice is also the highest in protein.

MISO NOODLE SOUP

This soup is a hybrid—the love child of chicken noodle and classic miso soup (in spirit, anyway, since this recipe does not actually include chicken). In my household, it has also become affectionately known as the "get-well soup," although we never wait around long enough to get sick to enjoy it!

MAKES 6 CUPS / 4 SERVINGS

2 Tbsp olive oil

1 medium yellow onion, finely diced

1 stalk celery, finely diced

1 large carrot, peeled and cut into ¼-inch slices

Sea salt and freshly ground black pepper

1 cup shiitake mushrooms, stemmed and thinly sliced

1 bay leaf

4 cups Miso Broth (page 63, or store bought), or more if needed, divided

1 cup soft tofu, cut into ¼-inch cubes

2 tsp dried wakame flakes

3 cups water

4 oz thin rice noodles

2 scallions, thinly sliced, for garnish

Minced fresh parsley, for garnish

Warm the oil in a large saucepan over moderate heat. Add the onion, celery, and carrot, and season with ¼ teaspoon of sea salt and a pinch of black pepper. Cook for 5 minutes to soften the vegetables, stirring occasionally. Stir in the mushrooms, bay leaf, and 2 cups of miso broth. Bring to a boil, then reduce the heat to low, cover, and cook for 20 minutes.

Reduce to the lowest heat on the stove and pour in the remaining 2 cups of miso broth and the tofu. Crumble the wakame flakes very finely over the soup (they will expand dramatically when hydrated), and gently mix them in. Cover the saucepan and keep it on the lowest heat for 5–10 minutes longer. If you prefer a thinner soup, add additional miso broth. Remove the bay leaf.

Just before serving, bring 3 cups of water to a boil. Place the thin rice noodles in a bowl, and pour the hot water on top. Let the bowl stand until the noodles are tender, about 3–5 minutes, then pour out the excess water. To serve, place a quarter of the rice noodles into each bowl. Fill the bowls generously with soup and scatter the tops with a few scallions and minced parsley.

SUPERFOOD TIP: If you're looking to make this soup in advance and store it, use 2 cups of another variety of cooked thin pasta (or brown rice), since rice noodles will get gummy when left to sit for long periods.

MINESTRONE WITH FARRO & CHIA PESTO

Instead of using pasta in this minestrone, I like to use farro (use whole, not pearled, farro here)—it adds a whopping 21 grams of protein! But what really makes this soup come alive is the addition of the fresh Chia Pesto, so definitely don't skip this essential ingredient.

MAKES 10 CUPS / 6 SERVINGS

1 large tomato, chopped

¼ cup dried goji berries

1 tsp kelp granules

8 cups Miso Broth (page 63, or store bought), divided

1 Tbsp olive oil

1 onion, chopped small

2 carrots, cut into thin half moons

2 stalks celery, chopped small

¾ cup farro

1 medium zucchini, chopped small

2 large cloves garlic, minced

1 Tbsp chopped fresh thyme

1 bay leaf

1 cup canned diced tomatoes with juice

1 tsp ground black pepper

1½ cups cooked garbanzo beans (page 13, or 1 15-oz can, drained)

½ lb broccoli florets, chopped small (about 3 cups)

3 big leaves kale, ribbed and chopped small

Sea salt

1 batch Chia Pesto (page 204), or ½ cup store-bought pesto

In a blender, combine the tomato, goji berries, and kelp granules with ½ cup of broth. Blend until smooth.

Warm the oil in a large heavy-bottomed pot over medium heat. Add the onion, carrots, celery, and farro, and cook, stirring often, for 6–7 minutes, or until the vegetables are softened. Add the zucchini, garlic, thyme, and bay leaf, and cook for 2 minutes longer, stirring constantly. Stir in the blended tomato mixture, the remaining 7½ cups of broth, the canned tomatoes with their juice, and the black pepper. Bring to a boil over high heat, then partially cover, leaving the lid a little ajar, and reduce the heat to medium-low. Simmer for 20 minutes. Turn up the heat to medium, stir in the garbanzo beans and broccoli, and cook, uncovered, for 10 minutes. Remove the mixture from the heat, and mix in the kale. Let the soup stand for 5–10 minutes to let the kale fully wilt. Remove the bay leaf, taste, and add salt as desired. To serve, ladle the soup into bowls and swirl in a tablespoon or two of Chia Pesto on top.

SUPERFOOD RAMEN BOWL

Ramen dishes don't have the healthiest reputation in the world (no thanks to some brands of packaged ramen that contain a mountain of sodium and strange additives that are definitely not good for you). Yet this distinctly superfood-infused recipe begs to differ, with many a trick up its sleeve. It really is a full meal in a bowl. The base, a mineral-rich antioxidant broth, is flecked with protein-packed black soybeans. Then come the ramen noodles: there are so many great options for these now, including gluten-free noodles and some that are made from ancient grains, like millet and brown rice. And finally, the ramen bowl is topped with crispy kale chips, which turn from crunchy to succulent the longer they sit atop the soup. You'll end up with a few more kale chips then you really need, but if an excess of kale chips is the worst problem you have in life, I think you can count yourself lucky.

MAKES 2 SERVINGS

- 1 bunch curly kale
- ¼ tsp garlic powder
- 1 Tbsp olive oil
- 3 Tbsp tamari, divided
- 2 cups Mushroom Broth (page 62, or store bought)
- 1 cup filtered water
- ⅛ tsp hickory liquid smoke
- 1 green tea bag
- 2 Tbsp dried goji berries
- 2 Tbsp dried yacon slices (optional)
- ¾ cup cooked black soybeans* (page 13, or half of a 15-oz can, drained)
- 1 Tbsp wakame flakes
- 2 tsp coconut oil
- 2 squares ramen noodles
- 2 green onions, white and light green parts, sliced thin

Preheat the oven to 275°F. Line two baking sheets with parchment paper or silicone baking mats.

Wash and dry the kale thoroughly. Strip away the stems and place the leaves in a large bowl, tearing apart any extra-large leaves. Sprinkle the kale leaves with garlic powder, olive oil, and 1 tablespoon of the tamari. Massage this marinade into the kale with your hands for about 1 minute, or until it is evenly distributed. Scatter the kale leaves evenly among the baking sheets, spreading the leaves apart as much as possible. Bake the kale on the center racks of the oven for 20–30 minutes, tossing the kale halfway through baking, until it is mostly crispy. Remove the kale from the oven and let it cool on the pan until you are ready to use it.

While the kale is cooking, in a medium saucepan, combine the remaining 2 tablespoons of tamari with the broth, water, liquid smoke, green tea bag, goji berries, yacon slices (if using), and black soybeans. Bring the mixture to a boil, and then reduce the heat to medium-low and gently simmer for 15 minutes. Remove the saucepan from the heat and remove the tea bag. Stir the wakame flakes and

coconut oil into the soup, cover the saucepan, and let it sit for a minimum of 15 minutes. Keep the soup warm until ready to serve.

Cook the ramen noodles according to the manufacturer's directions.

To serve, divide the cooked noodles into bowls, and ladle the soup on top. Pile the kale chips on top of the soup and garnish with green onions.

Note: Both the kale chips and the soup can be made far ahead of time. When you're ready to eat, simply warm up the soup and cook the noodles at the last minute.

* Black soybeans are an antioxidant-rich upgrade of their green cousins and taste like a cross between a regular soybean and a garbanzo bean. Though they are sold at most natural food stores, if you can't find them, use garbanzo beans instead.

PAD THAI NOODLE SOUP

This soup originated as a dinnertime peace treaty. My family was looking to soothe a pad Thai craving (as one sometimes gets), but bad weather meant it was a stay-in kind of night. I settled the grumbles by making a pot of pad Thai soup created entirely from ingredients we had on hand, and it was so good, we've been making versions of it ever since.

MAKES 4 SERVINGS

1 Tbsp coconut oil

½ yellow onion, finely chopped

2 cloves garlic, minced

3 carrots, shredded

½ lb broccoli, stem cut into matchsticks, florets cut small

1 Tbsp grated fresh ginger root

8 cups Seaweed Broth (page 64)

1 Tbsp yellow miso paste

3 Tbsp tamari

3 Tbsp coconut sugar

1 tsp Sriracha sauce, or more to taste

14 oz extra-firm tofu, drained and cut into ½-inch cubes

7 oz dried flat rice stick noodles

4 cups bean sprouts

¼ cup fresh lime juice

2 tsp dulse flakes, divided

4 green onions, white and light green parts only, sliced thin

¼ cup cilantro leaves

¼ cup slivered almonds

1 lime, quartered

Warm the coconut oil in a heavy-bottomed pot over medium heat. Add the onion and garlic, and cook for 2 minutes, stirring. Add the carrots and the broccoli stems and florets, and sauté until the broccoli is bright green, about 3 minutes longer, stirring often. Mix in the ginger and broth.

In a small bowl, whisk together the miso paste, tamari, coconut sugar, and Sriracha, making sure the miso dissolves, and then add this mixture to the soup. Turn the heat to high and bring to a boil. Stir in the tofu, noodles, bean sprouts, lime juice, and 1 teaspoon of the dulse flakes. Remove the pot from the heat and cover. Let the soup sit for 10 minutes, or until the noodles become tender, stirring once halfway through. To serve, ladle the soup into bowls, and top with green onions, cilantro leaves, almonds, the remaining dulse flakes, and lime wedges.

Note: *The lime wedge isn't just a garnish! Squeeze it over the soup to bring out its best flavors, right before eating.*

SUPERFOOD BOOST: Add 1 tablespoon of chia seeds when you stir in the noodles for brain-boosting fats.

KIMCHI DASHI BOWL WITH BUCKWHEAT NOODLES

Dashi is a seaweed broth simmered with dried fish flakes. To freshen things up, this version of the traditional recipe swaps out fish flakes and gives it an invigorating spin with mushrooms, ginger, and spicy kimchi (being a fermented food, kimchi is full of digestion-friendly enzymes). The buckwheat noodles alone offer 6 grams of protein per serving, and the bok choy and sesame seeds are both excellent sources of calcium. Dashi is a flexible recipe, and you can vary things by including other toppings like baked tofu, radishes, or extra seaweed to give this soup your own personal flair.

MAKES 4 SERVINGS

- 4 cups Seaweed Broth (page 64)
- 2 inches fresh ginger root, peeled and halved
- 1 Tbsp coconut sugar
- 1½ cups thinly sliced shiitake mushrooms
- 8 oz buckwheat soba (buckwheat pasta)
- 2 heads baby bok choy, halved lengthwise
- 1½ cups sugar snap peas, trimmed
- 2 green onions, white and light green parts only, sliced thin
- 1 Tbsp ume plum vinegar
- 2 tsp sesame oil
- ¼ cup kimchi, for serving
- ¼ cup kimchi juice (from jar), for serving
- 2 Tbsp toasted sesame seeds, for serving

Combine the Seaweed Broth, ginger, coconut sugar, and mushrooms in a large pot over high heat. Bring the mixture to a boil, then reduce the heat to a low simmer, and cook for 15 minutes.

While the broth is simmering, prepare the buckwheat noodles according to the manufacturer's directions.

After the broth has finished 15 minutes of simmering, discard the ginger pieces, and then add the bok choy and peas, submerging them in the broth. Cook for 3 minutes longer, until the vegetables are bright green and tender. Remove the pot from the heat and stir in the green onions, ume plum vinegar, and sesame oil.

To serve, divide the buckwheat noodles into four serving bowls. Transfer the vegetables to the bowls using tongs, and pour the broth on top. Place a small mound of kimchi in each bowl, and drizzle the top with kimchi juice. Sprinkle with sesame seeds and serve.

Variation: *You can also use quinoa, cooked in vegetable broth, in place of the buckwheat noodles.*

ONION SOUP WITH HEMP SEED PARMESAN

Thanks to much healthier ingredients, I can't call this a true French onion soup, but it still feels like a classic. The idea is to slow cook the onions until they fully caramelize, coaxing every last drop of flavor out of these wonderful humble ingredients.

MAKES 8 CUPS / 4 SERVINGS

2½ lbs yellow onions, peeled and quartered

2 Tbsp coconut oil

1 Tbsp apple cider vinegar

½ cup white wine

8 cups Mushroom Broth (page 62, or store bought)

2 bay leaves

2 Tbsp arrowroot flour

Sea salt and ground black pepper

4 slices sprouted bread,* toasted

1 recipe Hemp Seed Parmesan (page 213)

2 Tbsp minced chives

Thinly slice the quartered onions. Warm the oil over medium-low heat (err on the side of low), and then add the onions. Cook for 1 hour, stirring every few minutes, until the onions are evenly browned and caramelized—if the pan starts to scorch, reduce the heat, as the onions should be browned, not burned. Once the onions are fully caramelized, stir in the apple cider vinegar and the wine, and cook until the liquid has evaporated. Pour in the broth and add the bay leaves. Bring to a boil over high heat, then reduce the heat to medium-low and simmer for 15 minutes. Remove the bay leaves. Ladle ½ cup of the broth into a small bowl, and add the arrowroot flour, whisking to combine. Once the arrowroot is dissolved, add the mixture back into the soup, stirring to incorporate. Season with salt and pepper as desired.

Preheat the broiler. Ladle the soup into four ovenproof bowls and place them on top of a baking sheet. Slice the toasted bread into large croutons, and set them on top of the soup. Generously slice or sprinkle Hemp Seed Parmesan over the top of the soup, so that it is well covered. Place the pan in the oven to broil. Watch the soup closely, and remove it from the oven once the Parmesan is lightly browned, about 1–2 minutes. Sprinkle the soup bowls with chives and freshly ground black pepper, and serve.

* **Sprouted bread** is simply made from sprouted grains, which are higher in protein than unsprouted grains, and easier to digest, too. Most stores now carry sprouted grain bread, but if you can't find it, you can use slices of a traditional baguette in this recipe.

FARMERS MARKET SOUP

You never know what kind of organic and heirloom vegetables you'll find at the farmers market: rainbow carrots, baby turnips, purple spinach…the list goes on and on. And if you've been wondering what to do with any of that cool produce, this Farmers Market Soup is for you. All you have to do is pick a starchy vegetable, a leafy green, and a bundle of fresh herbs (suggestions below), and you're ready to enjoy this customizable, quick, and casual soup.

MAKES 10 CUPS / 6–8 SERVINGS

1 Tbsp olive oil

½ red onion, finely chopped

2 cloves garlic, minced

1 carrot, shredded

1 14-oz can salt-free chopped tomatoes, or 2 cups fresh chopped tomatoes

½ cup quinoa

2 cups starchy fresh vegetables*

1 Tbsp minced fresh herbs, or more to taste*

1½ cups cooked white beans (page 13, or 1 15-oz can, drained)

4 cups Vegetable Broth (page 60, or store bought)

2 summer squashes, spiralized into noodles, or shredded*

2 dozen Kalamata olives, pitted and chopped

3–4 cups torn leafy greens*

1 Tbsp red wine vinegar

Warm the oil in a heavy-bottomed pot over medium heat. Add the onion, garlic, and carrot, and cook 6–7 minutes to soften. Add the tomatoes and cook 5 minutes longer. Stir in the quinoa, starchy vegetables, fresh herbs, and white beans, and pour in the broth. Turn up heat to high, and bring to a boil. Cover, reduce the heat to medium-low, and cook 12 minutes.

Remove the cover and stir in the summer squash and olives. Cook for 2–3 minutes, until the squash is vibrant and tender, and then remove from the heat. Stir in the leafy greens and red wine vinegar and let sit until the greens have wilted. Adjust seasonings to taste, and stir in additional herbs if desired. Serve warm.

*SUGGESTIONS FOR FARMERS MARKET INGREDIENTS:
Example: yellow squash + corn + oregano + baby arugula

- **Starchy fresh vegetables:** New potatoes or diced turnips cut into ½-inch dice, sliced green beans, fresh peas, fresh corn kernels

- **Minced fresh herbs:** Oregano, thyme, marjoram, basil

- **Summer Squash:** Zucchini, yellow summer squash, small heirloom summer squashes

- **Leafy Greens:** Spinach, arugula, chard. You can also use stronger or more bitter, leafy greens, like dandelion or beet greens; just use a little bit less of them.

SPRINGTIME MINESTRONE

Spring always feels like a fresh start: a chrysalis that bursts with the earth's freshest offerings. This soup takes full advantage of spring's simple, clean flavors, and your taste buds will get an extra treat if you serve it with a few shavings of Hemp Seed Parmesan.

MAKES 7 CUPS / 4 SERVINGS

2 Tbsp olive oil, plus extra
  for serving

2 leeks, white and green parts,
  thinly sliced

3 small rainbow or regular carrots,
  thinly sliced

1 stalk celery, thinly sliced

2 cloves garlic, minced

¾ lb fingerling potatoes, cut
  into ¼-inch rounds

6 cups Vegetable Broth (page 60,
  or store bought)

2 cups fresh or frozen peas

1 Tbsp fresh lemon juice

¾ cup (packed) minced fresh
  parsley, divided

Sea salt

2 small radishes, thinly sliced

¼ cup Hemp Seed Parmesan
  (page 213) or toasted pine nuts

Warm the olive oil in a heavy-bottomed pot over medium heat. Add the leeks and cook for 2 minutes to soften. Add the carrots, celery, and garlic and cook for 5 minutes longer, stirring occasionally. Stir in the potatoes and broth. Bring the mixture to a boil over high heat, and then cover and reduce the heat to medium-low. Cook covered for 15–20 minutes, or until the potatoes are soft. Uncover the pot and stir in the peas, lemon juice, and ½ cup parsley. Cook the mixture for 2 minutes longer, or until the peas are bright green and tender, and then remove from the heat. Season the soup with salt to taste. To serve, ladle the soup into bowls, drizzle lightly with olive oil, and sprinkle generously with parsley, radish slices, and Hemp Seed Parmesan or toasted pine nuts.

SUPERFOOD BOOST: For extra protein, add ½ cup uncooked quinoa and 1 additional cup of broth while you're cooking the potatoes.

COCONUT CURRY SOUP

There's no need to make a takeout run when curry cravings arise. You can make your own! In addition to the flavorful broth and tender veggies, this bowl is topped, irresistibly, with crispy shallots and flaked coconut.

MAKES 8 CUPS / 4–6 SERVINGS

2 Tbsp coconut oil, divided

2 shallots, thinly sliced (about ½ cup)

⅓ cup shredded coconut (unsweetened)

Sea salt

2 garlic cloves, minced

1 Tbsp grated fresh ginger root

1 Tbsp Thai red curry paste

1 tsp curry powder

½ tsp ground coriander

½ tsp ground turmeric

6 cups Miso Broth (page 63 or store bought)

1 Tbsp dulse flakes

½ cup carrots, thinly sliced

1½ cups garbanzo beans (page 13 or 1 15-oz can)

3 cups chopped broccoli florets

1 13½-oz can full fat coconut milk

1 Tbsp tamari

2 Tbsp coconut sugar

1 cup snow peas, halved crosswise

3 cups baby spinach

⅓ cup cilantro, chopped

Lime wedges, for serving

Line a plate with a paper towel and set aside. Warm 1 tablespoon of the coconut oil in a heavy-bottomed pot over medium-high heat. Add the shallots and cook until well caramelized, stirring often, about 4–5 minutes. Add the coconut shreds and a pinch of salt and cook for 2–3 minutes longer, stirring constantly, until coconut is lightly browned. Transfer the contents of the pan to the prepared plate.

Return the pan to the stove and warm the remaining 1 tablespoon coconut oil over medium heat. Add the garlic, ginger, curry paste, curry powder, coriander, and turmeric, and cook for 30 seconds, stirring constantly. Add the miso broth, dulse flakes, carrots, and garbanzo beans, and bring to a boil. Cover, reduce heat to medium low, and cook for 5 minutes. Add the broccoli, coconut milk, tamari, and coconut sugar, and cook, uncovered, for 5 minutes longer. Stir in the snow peas, spinach, and cilantro, and cook until the spinach has wilted, about 1 minute. Remove from heat, ladle into bowls, and garnish with the fried shallot mixture and lime wedges.

Variation: *To add even more protein to this soup, add 2 cups of cubed firm tofu when you add the garbanzo beans, or serve the soup with a side of cooked quinoa or black rice.*

SUMMER SQUASH SOUP
WITH WASABI AVOCADO WHIP

Once upon a time, back when I was in college, I had a tiny studio while I pursued my dream of going to art school and refining my creative craft. Since most of my student budget went to fancy art supplies, I created the world's smallest "secret garden" in the back of my unit to supplement a diet that was otherwise largely dependent upon inexpensive grains. I was lucky—my tiny plot grew extremely well, and after my first summer I quickly became the master of all things zucchini. This humble soup is similar to one of my recipes from that period—and is still a favorite today. Very simple to prepare, the creamy avocado whip melts into the soup, making it balanced and alluring at the same time.

MAKES 6 CUPS / 4 SERVINGS

- 4½ cups Miso Broth (page 63, or store bought), divided
- 1½ tsp wasabi powder
- 1 large Hass avocado, pitted and peeled
- ¼ tsp sea salt
- 1 lb zucchini or yellow summer squash
- 1 Tbsp olive oil
- ½ yellow onion, finely diced
- 1 cup cooked brown rice
- 1½ cups cooked great northern beans, or cannelli beans (or 1 15-oz can, drained)
- 2 tsp dulse flakes
- 1 Tbsp toasted black sesame seeds
- ¼ cup microgreens, for garnish (optional)

In a food processor, combine ½ cup of the broth with the wasabi, avocado, and salt. Purée until smooth.

Use a spiralizer to transform the summer squash into noodles. Alternatively, simply julienne the squash into matchsticks.

Warm the olive oil in a heavy-bottomed pot over medium heat. Add the onion and cook for 7–8 minutes, until it is well caramelized. Stir in the summer squash and cook for 2 minutes longer, until the colors turn vibrant. Add the rice, beans, dulse, and the remaining 4 cups of broth, and cook for 5 minutes longer, over medium heat. To serve, ladle the broth into bowls and drizzle with avocado wasabi purée. Scatter the soup with sesame seeds, and top with a small nest of microgreens (if using).

SUPERFOOD BOOST: Add ½ teaspoon spirulina powder to the avocado mixture to enhance the soup's immune-boosting powers.

ROASTED ROOT & FARRO SOUP WITH APPLE SLAW

The first hint of spring is one of the most exciting times of the year. During the transition between seasons, I like to stick with warmer foods, but also yearn for a few cool delicacies—a little bit like wearing a sweater with flip-flops. This soup, with its variety of roasted roots, freshly made quick stock, and crunchy raw topping, is the culinary equivalent of that getup.

MAKES 6 CUPS / 4 SERVINGS

1 large yellow onion, quartered (unpeeled)

1 medium red apple, cored and finely chopped

2 stalks celery, cut into eighths

2 large garlic cloves, smashed (unpeeled)

2 tsp black peppercorns

2 tsp mustard seeds

2 bay leaves

½ bunch fresh parsley

2 medium fennel bulbs, cut into ¼-inch dice (about 3 cups), stems reserved, divided

Sea salt and ground black pepper

14 cups water

1 cup farro

4 carrots, cut into ¼-inch dice (2 cups)

2 Tbsp olive oil, divided

3 cups radishes (any variety), quartered or cut into bite-size pieces

Apple Slaw (page 212)

¼ cup chopped walnuts

Preheat the oven to 400°F.

Combine the onion, apple, celery, garlic, black peppercorns, mustard seeds, bay leaves, parsley, 1 cup of the chopped fennel, and all the fennel stems in a large stock pot. Add ½ teaspoon sea salt, and pour in the water. Over high heat, bring the mixture to a boil, then reduce the heat to a medium simmer and cook uncovered for 20 minutes.

Use a strainer to remove all the solids, yielding about 8 cups of stock. Pour the stock back into the stockpot and add the farro. Return the mixture to a boil and simmer for 30 minutes over medium heat until the farro is tender.

While the farro is cooking, place the carrots and remaining chopped fennel in a mixing bowl and toss with 1 tablespoon of olive oil, a couple of big pinches of salt, and a sprinkle of ground black pepper. Spread the mixture in a flat layer on a baking sheet. Next, toss the radishes with the remaining 1 tablespoon of olive oil and season with salt and pepper, as well. Spread the mixture on a second baking sheet. Place both sheets in the oven on the center racks, and cook for 20–22 minutes, tossing once halfway through, until the vegetables begin to caramelize. Once the farro is tender, add the roasted vegetables and simmer for 1 minute longer. If too much water has boiled away, add a bit more (the soup should be brothy and yield about 6 cups). Adjust seasonings to taste. Ladle the soup into bowls, divide the apple slaw on top, and sprinkle with walnuts.

CHOWDERS & PORRIDGES

Chowders and porridges are the types of dishes you just want to snuggle up with. They barely squeak into the category of soups, thanks to a creamy base wrapped around ample bits of chew, yet these full-bodied soups are some of the most nostalgic-feeling soup recipes of all. Whether you warm up a somber day with a batch of Roasted Cauliflower Chowder (page 163) or treat yourself to a bowl of simple Purple Yam & Buckwheat Porridge (page 165), you can enjoy a generous bowl of yum, any time of the day or week.

� = FEATURED SUPERFOOD INGREDIENT

✻ BEAUTY   ⬡ BONE STRENGTH   🍃 CLEANSE/DETOX

♥ HEART HEALTH   ✺ IMMUNITY   💧 LOW CALORIE   ⬡ PROTEIN

SPLIT PEA & HEMP SEED CHOWDER

This high-protein soup is packed with benefits like iron, fiber, and brain-boosting omega fats. Served with a salad, it makes an easy, satisfying, and balanced meal.

MAKES 8 CUPS / 6 SERVINGS

2 Tbsp coconut oil

1 medium yellow onion, diced

4 large cloves garlic, finely minced

2 carrots, finely chopped

2 celery stalks, finely chopped

2 bay leaves

1½ cups green split peas

3 Tbsp yellow miso paste

8 cups water

⅓ cup raw walnuts, chopped finely

½ cup hemp seeds

Sea salt and ground black pepper

In a large soup pot, heat the coconut oil over medium-high heat. Add the onion and cook for 2 minutes. Add the garlic, carrots, and celery, and cook for 3–4 minutes longer to soften the vegetables. Add the bay leaves, peas, miso paste, and water, and stir to combine. Cover, bring to a simmer, and then reduce the heat to medium-low. Cook for 50–60 minutes, stirring occasionally, until the peas have broken down, adding additional water if needed. Add the walnuts and the hemp seeds, and season with salt and pepper, if desired. Serve the soup warm, with plenty of freshly ground black pepper.

ARTICHOKE CHOWDER

If you use jarred artichoke hearts, this rewarding recipe comes together in a flash (jarred will taste much better than canned, in case you're wondering)—just be sure to use artichokes that are jarred in water, and not marinated in oil. Artichokes make a phenomenal chowder base, thanks to their succulent, chewy texture.

MAKES 6 CUPS / 4 SERVINGS

3 stalks celery, divided

1 Tbsp olive oil

1 Tbsp balsamic vinegar

Sea salt and ground black pepper

6 cups Miso Broth (page 63, or store bought), divided

1 Tbsp dulse flakes

½ cup raw cashews

2 Tbsp hemp seeds

1 Tbsp coconut oil

2 shallots, minced (½ cup)

2 cloves garlic, minced

1½ cups steamed artichoke hearts (or 1 14.5-oz jar in water, drained), chopped*

1 Tbsp cordyceps powder

2 Tbsp arrowroot powder

1 Tbsp fresh lemon juice

If there are any leaves on the celery, pull them off and set them aside for garnish. Finely chop two of the celery stalks and set aside. Mince the remaining celery stalk, and toss it with the olive oil, balsamic vinegar, ¼ teaspoon sea salt and ¼ teaspoon black pepper in a small bowl; set aside.

In a blender, combine 1 cup of broth with the dulse flakes, cashews, and hemp seeds. Blend until smooth. Turn off the machine, but keep the mixture in the blender while making the rest of the soup.

Warm the coconut oil in a heavy-bottomed pot over medium heat. Add the two reserved chopped celery ribs, shallots, and garlic and cook until softened, about 5 minutes. Pour in the remaining 5 cups of broth, and add the artichoke hearts and cordyceps powder. Bring the mixture to a boil over high heat, then reduce the heat to a simmer and cook for 10 minutes. Pour the soup into the blender with the cashew mixture, and add the arrowroot powder. Blend for just a moment—the soup should be partially puréed, while leaving bits of chewy texture. Return the soup to the pot and cook on low for an additional 3 minutes. Remove from heat and stir in the lemon juice. Adjust seasoning to taste. To serve, ladle the soup into bowls and top with a mound of the balsamic minced celery. Sprinkle a few drops of the balsamic liquid around the top of the soup and garnish with celery leaves.

* If you're making steamed artichokes fresh for this recipe, you'll need about 4–6, depending on how big they are.

CHEESY BROCCOLI SOUP

This soup comes very close to a traditional broccoli and cheese soup. My favorite way to serve it is to fully smother a freshly baked potato with its creamy goodness, sprinkle some hemp seeds on top, and call it dinner. You won't be disappointed!

MAKES 8 CUPS / 4 SERVINGS

2 Tbsp coconut oil

1 large yellow onion, finely chopped

2 garlic cloves, minced

1½ lbs broccoli, stems and florets separated, both finely chopped

1 lb cauliflower, finely chopped (about 4 cups)

8 cups Miso Broth (page 63, or store bought)

2 cups water, plus more as needed

¼ cup hemp seeds

2 Tbsp tahini

⅓ cup nutritional yeast

1 tsp smoked paprika

½ tsp ground black pepper

1 Tbsp ume plum vinegar

Warm the coconut oil in a heavy-bottomed pot over medium heat. Add the onion and garlic, and cook 3–4 minutes, stirring occasionally. Stir in the broccoli stems (not the florets) and the cauliflower and cook 3 minutes longer. Pour in the broth and water, and turn the heat up to high. Bring to a boil, and then reduce the heat to medium-low to a simmer. Cook the mixture for 15–20 minutes or until the cauliflower is very soft. Remove the pot from the heat and add the hemp seeds, tahini, nutritional yeast, paprika, and black pepper.

Transfer the mixture to a blender, working in batches if needed, and purée until smooth. Return the mixture to the pot (no need to clean the blender just yet). Add the broccoli florets to the soup, and bring it to a soft simmer over medium-low heat. Cover the pot, and cook for 10–15 minutes, or until the broccoli florets are tender.

Remove the pot from the heat, and stir in the ume plum vinegar. Return half of the soup to the blender, and briefly process, allowing some texture to remain. Stir puréed soup back into the pot. The soup should be thick, but it may be thinned with ¼ cup water at a time, as needed. Adjust seasonings, if desired, and serve the soup hot.

SUPERFOOD BOOST: To gain extra anti-inflammatory benefits and a boost of yellow color, add ¼ teaspoon turmeric powder while mixing in the spices.

OYSTER MUSHROOM CHOWDER
WITH COCONUT BACON BITS

Oyster mushrooms have a slight from-the-sea flavor but definitely taste more like fabulous mushrooms than actual oysters. If you can't find oyster mushrooms, substitute away with other types of fresh wild mushrooms for endless variations on this indulgent chowder.

MAKES 8 CUPS / 6 SERVINGS

⅔ cup raw cashews

6 cups Seaweed Broth (page 64), divided

2 Tbsp coconut oil

2 leeks, trimmed, halved, and thinly sliced

1 medium fennel bulb, finely chopped

2 ribs celery, finely chopped

4 cloves garlic, minced

¾ lb red potatoes, cut into ½-inch dice

1 fresh sprig rosemary

1 Tbsp cordyceps powder (optional)

6.5 oz oyster mushrooms, separated, trimmed, and chopped into large pieces (about 3 cups)

½ cup dry white wine

2 tsp dulse flakes

Sea salt and ground black pepper

½ cup Coconut Bacon Bits (page 209)

¼ cup minced parsley leaves

Combine the cashews with 2 cups of the broth in a blender. Blend until smooth. Set aside.

Warm the oil in a heavy-bottomed pot over medium heat. Add the leeks and cook for 2 minutes or until they are bright green and wilted. Stir in the fennel, celery, and garlic, and cook for 4–5 minutes longer to soften. Add the potatoes, rosemary, cordyceps powder (if using), and the last 4 cups of the broth. Bring the mixture to a boil over high heat, and then reduce the heat to medium-low, cover the pot, and simmer for 12–15 minutes, or until the potatoes are tender. Discard the rosemary sprig.

Add the mushrooms, wine, and blended cashew mixture to the pot. Over medium-low heat, return the soup to a simmer, and then cook for 5 minutes longer, or until the mushrooms are cooked through. Stir in the dulse flakes, and then season to taste with salt and pepper. To serve, ladle the chowder into bowls, and generously top with Coconut Bacon Bits and a sprinkle of parsley.

Variation: *If you're short on time, you can use almost-instant Miso Broth (page 63) in place of Seaweed Broth.*

ROASTED CAULIFLOWER CHOWDER

This homey soup is so recharging, thanks to its high-mineral ingredients like cauliflower and seagreens.

MAKES 8 CUPS / 4–6 SERVINGS

1 medium head cauliflower (about 1½ lbs)

3 Tbsp melted coconut oil, divided

Sea salt and ground black pepper

1 yellow onion, finely diced

4 stalks celery, finely diced

3 cloves garlic, minced

1 Tbsp fresh thyme leaves, minced

2 bay leaves

1 lb Yukon gold potatoes, cut into ½-inch dice

⅛ tsp cayenne pepper

5 cups Seaweed Broth (page 64)

2 Tbsp tahini

1 Tbsp fresh lemon juice

1 Tbsp dulse flakes, plus extra for garnish

¼ cup minced fresh chives, divided

¼ cup toasted pine nuts, for garnish

Preheat the oven to 400°F.

Trim away the coarse end and any leaves from the cauliflower. Chop the remaining florets and stem into small pieces—about the size of popcorn—and place in a large bowl; you should have about 8 cups. Toss the cauliflower with 2 tablespoons of the coconut oil, ½ teaspoon sea salt, and ¼ teaspoon ground black pepper. Spread the cauliflower on a baking sheet, and roast it for 25–28 minutes, stirring it once about halfway through cooking, until the cauliflower is well caramelized and small parts are crispy. Remove the cauliflower from the oven, and cover to keep warm.

While the cauliflower is roasting, warm the remaining 1 tablespoon coconut oil in a heavy-bottomed pot over medium heat. Add the onion and celery and cook until very soft, about 9–10 minutes, stirring occasionally. Stir in the garlic, thyme, and bay leaves, and cook 1 minute longer. Add the potatoes, cayenne, broth, ¼ teaspoon salt, and ¼ teaspoon black pepper. Turn up the heat to high, and bring to a boil. Reduce the heat to medium-low, partially cover the pot, and simmer for 15 minutes or until the potatoes are very soft. Turn the heat to low, and discard the bay leaves.

Ladle 2 cups of the soup into a blender, add the tahini and lemon juice, and blend until smooth. Pour the mixture back into the soup pot, along with the dulse flakes, 2 tablespoons of the chives, and the roasted cauliflower. Let the ingredients warm over low heat for about 2 minutes. Taste for seasoning, and serve the chowder with a generous sprinkle of pine nuts, chives, dulse flakes, and freshly ground black pepper.

INCA CHOWDER

Amaranth, chia, corn, beans, and potatoes were among the staple foods of the ancient Inca Empire… and judging by how well they get along in this simple blond-colored porridge-like chowder, this was a culture that really knew how to eat well! Though you can eat this soup right away, it gets even better with just a little bit of a wait, so I recommend letting it sit at least 30 minutes before serving.

MAKES ABOUT 7 CUPS / 4 SERVINGS

1 Tbsp coconut oil

1 leek, trimmed, halved, and thinly sliced

2 cloves garlic, minced

1 dried chile de árbol, finely crumbled, or ⅛ tsp cayenne pepper

1 bay leaf

½ lb Yukon gold potatoes, cut into ½-inch dice

⅓ cup amaranth

4 cups Vegetable Broth (page 60, or store bought)

1 tsp ground paprika

¼ tsp ground cinnamon

Sea salt and ground black pepper

Kernels cut from 2 ears of corn (1½ cups)

1½ cups cooked pinto beans (page 13, or 1 15-oz can, drained)

2 Tbsp chia seeds

2 Tbsp fresh lime juice

1 Tbsp maple syrup

4 scallions, white and light green parts sliced thin

2 Tbsp pepitas, chopped

Heat the oil in a large heavy-bottomed pot over medium heat. Add the leek and sauté for 3 minutes, stirring often, until bright green and softened. Mix in the garlic, chile de árbol, and bay leaf, and cook for 1 minute longer. Add the potatoes, amaranth, broth, paprika, cinnamon, ¼ teaspoon salt, and ¼ teaspoon ground black pepper. Over high heat, bring to a boil, then reduce the heat to low, cover, and cook for 15 minutes. Stir in the corn, cover again, and cook for 10 minutes longer. Add the beans, chia seeds, lime juice, maple syrup, and green onions. Simmer for 5 minutes, remove from the heat, and let the soup stand for 5 minutes longer to allow the amaranth and chia to fully swell. Remove the bay leaf, then taste and adjust seasonings as desired. Serve warm, topped with pepitas.

FEEL GOOD FACT: The Incas cultivated more than forty varieties of potatoes in all different colors and actually invented the idea of the dehydrated potato. Today, potatoes are the number one vegetable crop in the Untied States! More than just a comfort food, potatoes are also a great source of vitamin C (a medium potato contains almost half of our daily needs, as well as iron and potassium . . . and they are even surprisingly low in calories, too.

PURPLE YAM & BUCKWHEAT PORRIDGE

Breakfast, lunch, dinner, midnight snack—if this slightly sweet porridge is around, you best believe I'm reaching for another spoonful. Earthy, nutty cracked buckwheat is essentially hulled buckwheat groats that have been broken into bits—sometimes it's sold simply as "hot buckwheat cereal" (source listed in Ingredient Resources Guide on page 219). It makes a fantastic partner for heavy squashes and potatoes, or, in this case, purple Japanese yams. When roasted, these special yams taste almost like candy and are outstandingly rich in antioxidants, not to mention gorgeous to look at. If they're not available, you can also use regular yams or sweet potatoes in their place.

MAKES 4 SERVINGS

1 Tbsp coconut oil

1 lb Japanese purple yams (about 2 medium), peeled and cut into ¾-inch dice

Sea salt and ground black pepper

1 cup cracked buckwheat

5 cups unsweetened almond milk

1 cinnamon stick

1 Tbsp coconut sugar, plus extra for topping

2 tsp chia seeds

¼ cup hazelnuts, chopped

¼ cup unsweetened coconut flakes

Heat the oven to 400° F. Place the coconut oil on a baking sheet or large pan, and warm in the oven until the oil is melted, about 2–3 minutes. Remove the pan from the oven and add the yams. Sprinkle with ½ teaspoon sea salt and plenty of black pepper, toss well, and spread out the yams into an even layer on the pan. Cover tightly with aluminum foil and bake for 10 minutes. Remove the aluminum foil, toss the yams, cover once more, and return to the oven. Bake, for 5–10 minutes longer, or until the edges are well caramelized and the yams are very tender.

While the yams are cooking, combine the buckwheat, almond milk, cinnamon stick, and a pinch of salt in a large pot (the mixture will rise substantially while cooking). Over high heat, bring to a simmer, keeping a close eye while cooking so the milk doesn't bubble over. Once simmering, reduce heat to low, and cover, leaving the lid open just a crack; cook for 10 minutes. Remove from heat and discard the cinnamon stick. Stir in 1 tablespoon coconut sugar, and keep warm until ready to serve.

To serve, ladle porridge into bowls, and divide the roasted yams on top. Sprinkle with additional coconut sugar to taste, and top with chia seeds, hazelnuts, and coconut.

SORGHUM CORN CHOWDER

Sorghum and corn were absolutely made for each other—like two peas in a pod—and their flavors and textures complement each other perfectly in this toothsome, Southwestern-style soup. The recipe makes a fairly big batch, so if you think you won't get to all of it within a few days, fear not, as it can be frozen for later enjoyment and reheats very well.

MAKES 10 CUPS / 6–8 SERVINGS

3 ears corn, shucked

1¼ cup sorghum

1 bay leaf

11 cups water, divided

Sea salt and ground black pepper

2 Tbsp coconut oil

½ medium yellow onion, finely chopped

4 large cloves garlic, minced

1 Anaheim pepper, seeded and minced

½ lb zucchini, cut into ¼-inch dice

½ lb red potatoes, cut into ½-inch dice

¼ tsp cayenne pepper

½ cup raw cashews

1 Tbsp yellow miso paste

2 Tbsp arrowroot powder

2 Tbsp fresh lime juice

½ cup chopped fresh cilantro, divided

Cut the kernels from the corncobs, and set them aside in a bowl (you should have about 2¼ cups). Place the corncobs in a large heavy-bottomed pot, add the sorghum and bay leaf, and cover with 10 cups of the water. Bring to a boil, and then reduce the heat and simmer over medium heat for 45 minutes. Discard the cobs and bay leaf, and stir in ¾ teaspoon sea salt. Transfer the broth and sorghum to a large bowl or pitcher.

Return the pot to the stovetop and add the coconut oil over medium heat. Once the oil is hot, add the onion, and sauté for 5 minutes. Add the garlic and Anaheim pepper and cook, stirring often, for 2 minutes longer. Stir in the zucchini, along with the reserved corn kernels. Add a pinch of salt and ground black pepper, and cook for 5 minutes, tossing occasionally. Add the potatoes and the cayenne, as well as the sorghum with its broth. Bring the mixture to a boil over high heat, then reduce the heat to medium and simmer for 15 minutes, or until the potatoes are very soft.

In a blender, combine the cashews, miso, arrowroot, and remaining 1 cup of water. Blend until smooth, and stir into the soup. Return the soup to a boil, then simmer for 5 minutes longer to allow the arrowroot to thicken. Remove from the heat, and stir in lime juice and ¼ cup cilantro. Taste for seasoning, and adjust salt and pepper if desired. Ladle into soup bowls and top with additional cilantro.

RED LENTIL-CHIA PORRIDGE
WITH SHAVED RADICCHIO

Grab your most comfy sweatpants and sink into a bowl of this earnest goodness.
A protein-packed and super-hearty soup, this recipe is crazy easy to make,
and is essentially the poster child for why savory porridges rock.

MAKES 4 SERVINGS

1 Tbsp olive oil

1 medium yellow onion, finely chopped

1 carrot, finely chopped

4 cloves garlic, minced

½ cup red lentils

½ cup quinoa

2 tsp ground cumin

1 tsp ground turmeric

Pinch cayenne pepper

6 cups Vegetable Broth (page 60, or store bought)

Sea salt and ground black pepper

3 Tbsp fresh lemon juice

2 Tbsp chia seeds

½ small head radicchio, sliced paper-thin using a mandoline

2 Tbsp fresh minced parsley or cilantro leaves, for garnish

Warm the olive oil in a heavy-bottomed pot over medium heat. Add the onion, carrot, and garlic. Sauté, stirring occasionally, until the onion begins to turn translucent, about 5 minutes. Add the lentils, quinoa, cumin, turmeric, and cayenne, stirring to combine. Pour in the broth, add ¼ teaspoon ground black pepper, and turn the heat up to high. Bring to a boil, and then reduce the heat to medium-low. Simmer gently for 20 minutes or until the lentils are almost dissolved and the quinoa is very tender. Remove from the heat and stir in the lemon juice and chia seeds. Leave as a chunky soup, or blend partially (or entirely) for a more porridge-like texture. Season the mixture with salt and pepper to taste. Ladle into bowls, and top with a mound of radicchio and a few fresh herbs.

ZA'ATAR AMARANTH PORRIDGE

Amaranth gives soup a wonderful porridge-like texture. Here, it is offset with chunks of melt-away potatoes, sweet corn, savory chickpeas, and wilted arugula. But the real star of the show is the za'atar seasoning (page 203), which elevates an otherwise humble soup to the height of second-helping heaven with its woodsy-tart flair.

MAKES 6 CUPS / 4 SERVINGS

1 Tbsp olive oil

½ yellow onion, finely chopped

2 cloves garlic, minced

1 medium russet potato, peeled and cut into ½-inch dice

1 Tbsp + 1 tsp za'atar (page 203), divided

¾ cup amaranth

4 cups Vegetable Broth (page 60, or low-sodium store bought)

1½ cups cooked garbanzo beans (page 13, or 1 15-oz can, drained)

1 cup frozen corn kernels, thawed

1 Tbsp fresh lemon juice

3 cups baby arugula

Sea salt and ground black pepper

2 Tbsp tahini paste

Ground sumac, for garnish (optional)

Warm the olive oil in a heavy-bottomed pot over medium heat. Add the onion and garlic and sauté for 5 minutes, stirring occasionally, until the onion begins to turn translucent. Add the potato, 1 tablespoon of the za'atar, and amaranth, and cook for 1 minute, stirring constantly. Pour in the broth and increase the heat to high. Bring the soup to a boil, cover, and reduce the heat to medium-low. Simmer for 15 minutes. Stir in the garbanzo beans and corn. Simmer, uncovered, for 10 minutes longer. Remove from the heat, and stir in the lemon juice and arugula, until the leaves are wilted.

Just before serving, in a small bowl, combine the tahini paste and remaining 1 teaspoon za'atar. Add a little bit of water (amount will vary based on the thickness of the tahini paste—start with a couple of tablespoons) to the bowl, and whisk the mixture into a sauce that can easily be drizzled. Stir 1 tablespoon of this sauce into the pot, and adjust the final seasoning of the porridge, if desired. To serve, ladle the porridge into bowls and drizzle the additional tahini sauce and a generous sprinkle of ground sumac to garnish.

FREEKEH PORRIDGE WITH SHIITAKE & KALE

Your new weeknight superfood supper has arrived! If time is of the essence, you can make the freekeh porridge a few days in advance (on a lazy Sunday, let's say), and just reheat it with a little broth while you're whipping up the quick mushroom and kale topping for this tasty dish. Voilà! Supper in 15 minutes.

MAKES 4 SERVINGS

5 cups Mushroom Broth (page 62, or store bought), divided use, plus more as needed

1 cup freekeh

2 Tbsp tamari

3 Tbsp olive oil, divided

2 large cloves garlic, minced

6 large curly kale leaves, stemmed and finely chopped

Sea salt and ground black pepper

1 cup shallots, thinly sliced

8 oz shiitake mushrooms, thinly sliced (about 6 cups)

2 Tbsp apple cider vinegar

¼ cup hemp seeds

2 radishes, shaved thin

Combine 4 cups of the broth along with the freekeh in a medium saucepan. Over medium heat, bring the mixture to a gentle boil. Cover the saucepan, and reduce the heat to low; let the mixture simmer (without stirring it) for 30 minutes. Remove the saucepan from the heat and let it sit, still covered, for 15 minutes longer, to allow it to steam and soften further.

Pour 1 cup of the cooked freekeh (mixture will be brothy) as well as the remaining 1 cup of the broth into a blender. Purée until smooth, and then stir the blend back into the porridge, along with the tamari. Keep the porridge warm over the lowest heat, adding additional broth, as needed, to create a thick, soupy texture.

Warm 1 tablespoon of the olive oil in a large sauté pan. Add the garlic and sauté for 30 seconds. Stir in the kale and a pinch of salt. Cook, stirring constantly, until the kale is bright green and wilted. Transfer the garlic and kale mixture to a covered dish to keep it warm. Return the sauté pan to the stove and warm the remaining 2 tablespoons of oil. Add the shallots and cook for 2 minutes, stirring, to soften. Stir in the mushrooms, as well as a pinch of salt and ground black pepper to taste. Add the apple cider vinegar and cook the mushrooms, stirring constantly, for 3–4 minutes longer, until the mushrooms are very tender. Remove the pan from the heat. Ladle the porridge into serving bowls and top with a layer of kale and mushrooms. Sprinkle hemp seeds and scatter shaved radishes on top of each bowl.

TURMERIC-WALNUT QUINOA PORRIDGE

Now, this is what I call an instant meal! Seriously, this delicious, extra-homey, anti-inflammatory, and protein-packed porridge comes together in 5 minutes, and once you become addicted to it (join the club), try one of the variations below. Although this porridge makes a great quick lunch or dinner, you can also enjoy it as a warm start to your morning, if you enjoy savory breakfasts as much as I do.

MAKES 5 CUPS / 4 SERVINGS

- 4 cups Vegetable Broth (page 60, or store bought)
- ½ tsp ground turmeric
- 1 cup quinoa flakes
- 1½ cups baby spinach, thinly sliced
- 1 Tbsp coconut oil
- 1½ Tbsp nutritional yeast
- 1½ Tbsp tamari
- ¼ cup walnuts, chopped
- ⅛ tsp ground black pepper
- 3 Tbsp hemp seeds, divided

In a medium saucepan, bring the broth and turmeric to a rapid boil. Stir in the quinoa flakes, return to a boil, and cook for 90 seconds, stirring often. Remove the saucepan from the heat and stir in the spinach, coconut oil, nutritional yeast, tamari, walnuts, ground black pepper, and 2 tablespoons of the hemp seeds. Let the porridge sit for 1 minute, then ladle it into bowls and top with the 1 tablespoon of remaining hemp seeds.

Variations: *Turmeric-Walnut Quinoa Porridge should really be called "accoutrement porridge," because it goes with just about everything. For example, simply stir a healthy spoonful of any great superfood sauce—Chia Pesto (page 204), Green Harissa (page 205), and Goji Harissa (page 206) all work exceptionally well—into the base of vegetable broth and quinoa flakes to make a stunning bowl of goodness. Or stir a handful of chopped leafy greens into the mix and top with your favorite seeds and nuts for a go-to, fully personalized porridge bowl that's super easy to make and totally satisfying!*

KITCHARI

✳ ◐ ◖ ♥ ✺ ◌ ⬡

Kitchari, a famous mixture used in Ayurvedic medicine, usually includes a starch, in the form of grains, and a protein, in the form of legumes. The recipe is used to balance the body in myriad ways—to detoxify, ease digestion, balance weight, and support recovery from illness or physical hardship. Some people even make huge batches of kitchari at a time to use as a base for cleanses. Regardless of how you enjoy it, kitchari is considered the ultimate in feel-good porridges.

MAKES 7 CUPS / 4 SERVINGS

2 Tbsp coconut oil

1 tsp cumin seeds

1 tsp fennel seeds

1 tsp black mustard seeds

1 cup long grain brown rice

½ cup yellow split peas

1 tsp ground coriander

⬜ ½ tsp ground turmeric

⬜ 1 tsp freshly grated ginger

6 cups water

⬜ 1 2×4-inch strip kombu

⬜ 1 Tbsp chaga powder (optional)

Sea salt

1 cup finely chopped carrots

2 cups finely chopped cauliflower

⬜ 4 medium Swiss chard leaves, finely chopped, stems and leaves chopped separately (about 2 cups total yield)

⬜ ¼ cup chopped fresh cilantro (optional)

Warm the coconut oil in a heavy-bottomed pot over medium heat. Once hot, add the cumin seeds, fennel seeds, and black mustard seeds. Cook, stirring, until the mustard seeds begin to pop and the spices are fragrant, about 2–3 minutes. Stir in the brown rice, yellow peas, coriander, turmeric, and ginger and cook for 1 minute longer, stirring constantly so as not to burn the spices. Pour in 6 cups of water and add the kombu strip, chaga powder (if using), and 1¼ teaspoons sea salt. Bring the mixture to a boil over high heat. Cover, reduce the heat to medium-low, and cook for 30 minutes.

Stir in the carrots, cauliflower, and chopped Swiss chard stems, adding more water as needed. Cover the pot again, and cook for 30 minutes longer, or until the vegetables, rice, and peas are very soft. Stir in the chard leaves and adjust the seasonings if needed, adding more water if a more soupy consistency is desired. Remove the soup from the heat and let rest until the chard is tender. Serve the soup warm with a little chopped cilantro.

Variation: *Kitchari is immensely flexible in its ingredients and structure. You can use anywhere from 2 to 6 cups of any vegetable you enjoy in this recipe, such as zucchini and green beans. You can even swap out the rice for another starch and the peas for another legume.*

STEWS & CHILIS

Although the difference between a hearty, chunky soup and a stew or a chili may be blurry, one thing is abundantly clear: no matter what you call them, these types of recipes are the very definition of soulfully satisfying. Plunge your spoon into the recipes in this chapter, and you'll see just how rewarding and delicious they truly are. With complex flavors and a meal-in-a-bowl mentality, you'll find protein-rich recipes like Cauliflower-Chia Chili, and beautifully spiced creations like Moroccan Harira Stew. Once your soup pot is on the stove, the only rule to follow is your hungry instinct.

�֍ = FEATURED SUPERFOOD INGREDIENT

✳ BEAUTY ◉ BONE STRENGTH 🍃 CLEANSE/DETOX

♥ HEART HEALTH ✺ IMMUNITY ◊ LOW CALORIE ⬡ PROTEIN

PORTOBELLO BARLEY SOUP
WITH HORSERADISH CREAM

Between the chewy, meaty texture of barley and Portobello mushrooms, and the smoothness of chia seeds (which also offer a big protein and fiber boost), there is something so earnest about this toothsome soup. A generous drizzle of horseradish cream adds a little pizzazz, like signing your name using a glitter pen.

MAKES 6 CUPS / 4 SERVINGS

1 Tbsp coconut oil

½ medium yellow onion, finely chopped

1 carrot, thinly sliced

1 stalk celery, thinly sliced

½ lb portobello mushrooms, chopped into ½-inch dice

2 cloves garlic, minced

1 tsp fresh thyme leaves

½ cup barley

¼ cup chia seeds

6 cups Mushroom Broth (page 62, or store bought)

2 Tbsp tamari

¼ cup Horseradish Cream (page 202)

¼ cup finely chopped flat-leaf parsley, for garnish

Warm the coconut oil in a heavy-bottomed pot over medium heat. Add the onion, carrot, and celery, and cook until slightly softened, about 3–4 minutes. Add the mushrooms, garlic, and thyme, and cook for 3–4 minutes longer, stirring often. Add the barley, chia seeds, broth, and tamari. Bring the mixture to a boil over high heat, and then reduce the heat to a low simmer and cover. Cook for 25–30 minutes, or until the barley is tender. Adjust the seasonings as desired, and serve the soup warm, generously drizzled with Horseradish Cream and topped with fresh parsley.

SUPERFOOD BOOST: Add 1 tablespoon of your favorite superfood mushroom powder, such as reishi, cordyceps, or chaga, when you add the mushroom broth.

CAULIFLOWER-CHIA CHILI

This lower calorie chili has a gorgeous depth of flavor thanks to a special secret ingredient: cacao.

MAKES 12 CUPS / 6 SERVINGS

- ⅓ cup chia seeds
- 1 28-oz can diced tomatoes
- 1 Tbsp chipotle powder
- 2 cups water
- ½ head cauliflower (about ½ lb)
- 3 Tbsp coconut oil
- 1 yellow onion, finely diced
- 1 green bell pepper, finely diced
- 2 carrots, finely diced
- 4 cloves garlic, minced
- 1 Tbsp chili powder
- 1 Tbsp ground cumin
- 1 Tbsp dried oregano
- 2 Tbsp cacao powder
- 1 Tbsp tamari
- 2 cups frozen corn kernels, thawed
- 1½ cups cooked kidney beans (page 13, or 1 15-oz can, drained)
- 1½ cups cooked garbanzo beans (page 13, or 1 15-oz can, drained)
- Sea salt
- ½ cup Cashew Sour Cream (page 210, or sour cream of choice)
- Cilantro leaves, for serving
- Chopped scallions, for serving

In a medium bowl, combine the chia seeds, diced tomatoes and their juices, chipotle powder, and water. Mix well to incorporate the seeds, and set aside.

Chop the cauliflower into florets, and place in a food processor. Pulse several times to grind the cauliflower into bits about the size of rice.

Warm the coconut oil in a heavy-bottomed pot over medium heat. Add the onion, bell pepper, carrots, and garlic. Cook for 5 minutes, stirring occasionally. Add the ground cauliflower along with the chili powder, cumin, oregano, cacao powder, and tamari, and cook for 3 minutes longer, stirring constantly. Pour in the tomato-chia mixture, and mix in the corn, kidney beans, garbanzo beans, and ½ teaspoon sea salt. Bring to a boil over high heat, and then reduce the heat to low to gently simmer. Cook for 45–60 minutes, stirring occasionally, until the vegetables are tender but retain a little texture. Remove from the heat, and adjust seasoning as desired. Serve with a generous dollop of sour cream, cilantro, and green onions.

RED LENTIL & COCONUT DAL STEW

✳ ◖ ♥ ✸ ⬡

Cooked way, way down, the lentils melt away into a creamy, aromatic stew base—the perfect complement to the varied textures of chia seeds, garbanzo beans, and spinach.

MAKES 8 CUPS / 4 SERVINGS

3 Tbsp coconut oil

1 medium yellow onion, finely diced

6 cloves garlic, minced

2 Tbsp grated fresh ginger root

1 tsp cumin seeds

2 tsp garam masala

1 tsp ground turmeric

1 cup red lentils

3 Tbsp chia seeds

4 cups Vegetable Broth (page 60, or store bought)

1 cup water

Sea salt and ground black pepper

1 13.5-oz can light coconut milk

1½ cups cooked garbanzo beans (page 13, or 1 15-oz can)

2 cups (packed) baby spinach

3 Tbsp fresh lemon juice, divided

½ cup unsweetened coconut yogurt (or other unsweetened non-dairy yogurt), for serving

½ tsp ground sumac, for serving

2 Tbsp cilantro leaves, for serving (optional)

Warm the oil in a large pot over medium heat. Add the onion and sauté for 5 minutes, stirring occasionally. Mix in the garlic, ginger, cumin seeds, garam masala, and turmeric, and cook for 1 minute longer, stirring constantly so as not to burn the spices. Add the lentils and chia seeds, stir to coat them with oil, then pour in the vegetable broth and water. Season with ¼ teaspoon sea salt and ¼ teaspoon of ground black pepper. Turn the heat up to high, and bring the mixture to a boil, then reduce the heat to medium-low to keep the stew at a simmer. Cook for 25-30 minutes, or until the mixture is fairly thick and the lentils are almost dissolved, stirring occasionally. Add the coconut milk, garbanzo beans, and spinach. Return the soup to a simmer over medium-low heat, and simmer until ingredients are heated through and spinach is wilted. Remove the stew from the heat and mix in 2 tablespoons of the lemon juice. Taste for seasoning, and adjust the salt and pepper as desired. Keep warm.

In a small bowl, whisk together the yogurt with the remaining 1 tablespoon lemon juice, plus ⅛ teaspoon salt. Ladle the stew into bowls, and garnish with a drizzle of yogurt, a sprinkle of sumac, and a few cilantro leaves.

SUPERFOOD BOOST: Add 2 tablespoons dried goji berries after adding the water.

CHILI CON NUECES

Chili with nuts! Ground walnuts, as well as hemp seeds, give this extra-hearty chili incredible texture.

MAKES 10 CUPS / 8 SERVINGS

2 cups raw walnuts

2 cups chopped crimini mushrooms

1 28-oz can unsalted diced tomatoes

1 chile in adobo sauce, plus 3 Tbsp adobo sauce*

6 Tbsp dried goji berries, divided

2 Tbsp yellow miso paste

2 Tbsp tomato paste

1 Tbsp dried oregano

1 Tbsp ground cumin

4 Tbsp chili powder

1 tsp ground cinnamon

3 Tbsp olive oil

2 large onions, minced

1 green bell pepper, minced

4 cloves garlic, minced

¼ cup hemp seeds

1 cup red wine

1 cup water

1½ cups cooked black beans (page 13, or 1 15-oz can, drained)

1½ cups cooked kidney beans (page 13, or 1 15-oz can, drained)

1 Tbsp maple syrup

Sea salt

Cashew Sour Cream (page 210)

Lime wedges, for serving

In a food processor, use the pulse function to briefly grind the walnuts into small bits, about the size of gravel or ground beef—be sure not to overprocess or the walnuts will become a fine flour. Transfer the walnuts to a bowl. Place the mushrooms in the food processor, pulse a few times until they're diced, and then transfer them to the bowl with the walnuts.

Add the tomatoes to the food processor along with the chile and adobo sauce, goji berries, yellow miso paste, tomato paste, oregano, cumin, chili powder, and cinnamon. Process briefly into a chunky mixture, stopping the machine and scraping down the sides if needed.

Warm the oil in a large, heavy-bottomed pot over medium heat. Add the onions and bell pepper, and sauté for 5 minutes. Stir in the garlic, hemp seeds, and the walnut and mushroom mixture, and cook for 2 minutes, stirring constantly. Add the blended tomato mixture and cook down slightly for 4–5 minutes, stirring often to prevent burning. Pour in the red wine, water, black beans, kidney beans, and maple syrup. Return the mixture to a simmer, and then reduce the heat to low. Cover, leaving the lid open a slight crack, and simmer for 1 hour, stirring occasionally. Let the chili cool for a couple of minutes, then taste for seasoning and adjust salt if desired. Serve warm, topped with Cashew Sour Cream and a squeeze of fresh lime.

* You can usually find this inexpensive canned ingredient in the area of your supermarket where Mexican foods are sold.

AFRICAN MINESTRONE STEW

Although this recipe takes a rather liberal approach to true West African food, I think it gets the essence across: delicious.

MAKES ABOUT 9 CUPS / 4–6 SERVINGS

1 Tbsp coconut oil

1 onion, finely diced

1 stalk celery, finely diced

1 carrot, finely diced

2 cloves garlic, minced

1 Tbsp fresh thyme, chopped

¼ cup tomato paste

1 14.5-oz can fire-roasted diced tomatoes

8 cups water

4 cups Miso Broth (page 63, or store bought)

1 cup dried black-eyed peas

¼ tsp cayenne pepper

½ tsp ground allspice

Sea salt and ground black pepper

½ lb green beans, trimmed and cut into 1-inch pieces

1 lb sweet potatoes, peeled and cut into ½-inch dice

¼ cup smooth almond butter

⅓ cup pineapple juice

4 cups (packed) baby spinach

¼ cup chopped cilantro, plus more for serving

¼ cup Candied Seed Clusters (page 211) or slivered almonds, for serving

Warm the oil in a large heavy-bottomed pot over medium heat. Add the onion, celery, and carrot, and cook until soft and caramelized, about 10 minutes. Add the garlic and thyme and cook for 1 minute longer. Stir in the tomato paste and cook until it begins to darken, about 2 minutes. Add the canned tomatoes, water, miso broth, black-eyed peas, cayenne, and allspice, and season with ¼ teaspoon sea salt and a full teaspoon of ground black pepper.

Over high heat, bring the mixture to a boil, and then reduce the heat to medium-low and simmer for 15 minutes. Add the green beans and sweet potatoes, and return to a simmer. Cook the mixture, uncovered, for 45 minutes longer, or until the black-eyed peas are tender.

Whisk together the almond butter and pineapple juice, and then stir the mixture into the soup, along with the spinach and cilantro. Cook for 5 minutes and then remove the pot from the heat. Adjust seasonings as desired. Let the stew rest for 5–10 minutes before serving warm, generously garnished with Candied Seed Clusters and additional chopped cilantro.

CACAO BLACK BEAN SOUP

The secret to this stewy soup is the combination of rustic earthiness and exotic sour, spicy, smoky, and sweet highlights. The recipe is, in fact, heavily inspired by mole, the classic savory Mexican sauce that includes chocolate (as well as a laundry list of other ingredients), but it leans more toward a classic black bean soup that just happens to have serious attitude more than anything else. On the scale of spicy soups, this one is about a medium, but if you're a card-carrying heat lover, go ahead and blend in a second chipotle chile.

MAKES 6 CUPS / 4 SERVINGS

2 Tbsp olive oil

1 white onion, finely chopped

1 stalk celery, finely chopped

1 carrot, finely chopped

2 large cloves garlic, minced

3 cups cooked black beans (page 13, or 2 15-oz cans, drained)

6 cups water

2 Tbsp yellow miso paste

1 chipotle chile in adobo sauce plus 1 Tbsp adobo sauce*

2½ Tbsp cacao powder

2 Medjool dates, pitted

1 Tbsp almond butter

½ tsp dried oregano

1 tsp ground cumin

¼ tsp ground allspice

½ tsp ground black pepper

¼ cup fresh lime juice (about 2 limes)

Sea salt

¼ cup Cashew Sour Cream (page 210, or store-bought sour cream)

¼ cup chopped fresh cilantro

Warm the oil in a heavy-bottomed pot over medium heat. Add the onion, celery, carrot, and garlic and cook for 10 minutes, stirring occasionally, to lightly brown the vegetables. Add the black beans and water, stirring to combine. Ladle 1½ cups of soup—the liquid, beans, and vegetables—into a blender. To the blender, add the miso paste, chipotle chile and sauce, cacao powder, dates, almond butter, oregano, cumin, allspice, and black pepper. Purée the mixture until it is smooth, and then pour it back into the soup. Turn the heat up to high and bring the soup to a boil, and then reduce the heat to medium-low and simmer for 30 minutes, uncovered, stirring occasionally.

Once the soup is cooked, check the consistency (different batches of beans can produce slightly different results); if the soup is too thin, simmer it for another 10–15 minutes until it has cooked down and thickened. Remove it from the heat and stir in the lime juice. Taste for seasoning, adding salt if desired. Serve the soup with Cashew Sour Cream and chopped cilantro.

* Sold canned.

BLACK LENTIL PORTOBELLO STEW
WITH CELERIAC PURÉE

Somehow, this stew feels delightfully Gothic to me, with its dark palette, meaty and earthy flavors, and woodsy notes. Perhaps it is no coincidence that it was created after I came home, ravenously hungry, from a winter hike in the mountains, and in need of a comforting and hearty fix—quick.

MAKES 6 CUPS/ 4 SERVINGS

- 5 large red Swiss chard leaves
- 2 Tbsp coconut oil, divided
- ½ red onion, diced
- 3 cloves garlic, minced
- 1 cup fruity red wine, like merlot
- 2 large Portobello mushrooms, cut into ½-inch dice
- ¾ cup dried black lentils
- ¼ cup dried goji berries
- 1 small sprig fresh rosemary
- 4 cups Mushroom Broth (page 62, or store bought)
- ½ cup water
- 1 Tbsp red wine vinegar
- Sea salt and ground black pepper
- ½ lb celeriac (celery root), peeled and cut into ½-inch dice (about 2 cups)
- ⅓ cup walnuts
- Torn radicchio leaves, for garnish (optional)

Strip the chard leaves away from the thick stems. Slice the leaves thinly (chiffonade), and set aside. Chop the stems finely and place with the onions.

Heat 1 tablespoon of the coconut oil in a heavy-bottomed pot over medium heat. Add the chopped chard stems, onion, and garlic, and sauté for 5 minutes. Add the red wine and mushrooms, and simmer for 5 minutes longer. Add the lentils, goji berries, rosemary, broth, and water, and turn the heat up to high. Bring the mixture to a boil, and then cover, leaving the lid slightly ajar, and reduce the heat to medium-low. Simmer for 30 minutes.

Remove the cover from the stew after 30 minutes, and add the chard leaves. Cook for 5 minutes longer, and then remove from the heat and stir in the red wine vinegar. Cover the pot, and let the soup stand for a minimum of 20 minutes before serving to allow the chard to fully tenderize and the flavors to further meld (the soup tastes better the longer it sits). Season to taste with salt and pepper, and add additional water if a thinner stew is desired.

While the stew is sitting, make the purée. Place the celeriac in a small saucepot and cover with a couple of inches of water. Add a generous pinch of salt. Bring the water to a boil and cook until very tender, about 20 minutes. Reserve ½ cup of the cooking water and

drain the remaining liquid. Transfer the celeriac to a blender and add the reserved water, walnuts, the remaining 1 tablespoon of coconut oil, and ¼ teaspoon sea salt. Purée the mixture until it is smooth, and set aside.

Rewarm the stew gently as needed. To serve, ladle the stew into bowls, swirl in the celeriac purée, and garnish with a couple of radicchio leaves.

SUPERFOOD BOOST: Add 1 tablespoon of your favorite superfood mushroom powder when adding the broth to the stew. (See page 18 for information about mushroom powders.)

TOMATO-TEMPEH STEW

Crumbled tempeh offers a hearty texture that perfectly complements the tomatoes in this rich and aromatic stew. Blending just a portion of the mixture helps create a creamier base without adding additional oil or cream.

MAKES 6 CUPS / 4 SERVINGS

1 Tbsp olive oil

½ large sweet onion, finely chopped

3 cloves garlic, minced

1 small fennel bulb, finely chopped (about 1 cup)

8 oz tempeh, finely crumbled

1 Tbsp fresh thyme leaves

½ tsp fennel seeds

2 tsp dulse flakes

1 14-oz can chopped tomatoes, including liquid

2 Tbsp tomato paste

4 cups Vegetable Broth (page 60, or store bought)

½ cup unsweetened almond milk

Sea salt and ground black pepper

¼ cup fresh basil, thinly sliced

½ cup Sprouted Croutons (page 214), for garnish (optional)

Warm the olive oil in a heavy-bottomed pot over medium heat. Add the onion, garlic, and fennel, and cook until translucent, about 5 minutes. Stir in the tempeh, thyme, and fennel seeds. Cook for 3–4 minutes longer, stirring often, until the vegetables have softened.

Add the dulse, canned tomatoes, and tomato paste, and stir well to combine. Pour in the vegetable broth. Bring to a boil over high heat, then reduce the heat to medium-low, and simmer for 40 minutes.

Remove from heat, and ladle 1 cup of hot soup into a blender and blend until very smooth. Pour the puréed soup back into the soup pot, mix in the almond milk, and adjust seasonings as desired. Top soup with basil just before serving, and toss a few croutons on top.

MOROCCAN HARIRA STEW

Harira is arguably the most famous soup in Morocco. Although it's traditionally made with lamb, the tantalizing spices and protein-rich legumes easily stand up on their own, as proven in this exotic-tasting and exceptionally satisfying plant-based riff. Some of the ingredients may seem a little unusual for a stew (such as cinnamon and figs), but you'll be amazed at how well the flavors fold together in the end. With a small salad on the side, this stew makes a wonderful meal.

MAKES 10 CUPS / 6 SERVINGS

1 Tbsp olive oil

1 large onion, finely chopped

4 stalks celery, finely chopped

4 cloves garlic, minced

1 tsp ground cinnamon

1 tsp ground turmeric

1 tsp grated fresh ginger root

½ cup chopped fresh parsley

½ cup chopped fresh cilantro, plus extra for garnish

1 28-oz can unsalted diced tomatoes

12 pitted green olives, minced

12 dried Turkish figs, finely chopped

1½ cups cooked garbanzo beans (page 13, or 15-oz can, drained)

1 cup black lentils

7 cups Vegetable Broth (page 60, or store bought)

Sea salt and ground black pepper

2 Tbsp fresh lemon juice

Warm the oil in a heavy-bottomed pot over medium heat. Add the onion and celery, and sauté for 7–8 minutes, or until the vegetables are softened but not brown. Add the garlic, cinnamon, and turmeric, and cook for 1 minute, stirring constantly. Add the ginger, parsley, and cilantro, and continue to stir for 30 seconds longer. Add the tomatoes, olives, figs, garbanzo beans, lentils, broth, ½ teaspoon of salt, and ½ teaspoon ground black pepper. Turn the heat to high and bring the mixture to a boil. Cover the pot, leaving the lid open just a crack, and reduce the heat to medium-low to simmer. Cook the mixture for 30–35 minutes, or until the lentils are very tender and soft. Remove the pot from the heat. Stir in the lemon juice, and then adjust salt to taste. Serve the stew warm, with a couple of cilantro leaves as garnish.

SUPERFOOD BOOST: To give the stew the benefit of an extra hit of carotene and lycopene antioxidants, toss in ¼ cup dried goji berries with an extra ¼ cup of Vegetable Broth when you add the lentils.

PERUVIAN QUINOA STEW

Long, long (I mean, like, embarrassingly long) before quinoa hit the mainstream health movement in North America, quinoa had enjoyed a storied history in Central and South American kitchens as an inexpensive, profoundly nourishing, and environmentally friendly protein. One of quinoa's many famous uses is in sopa de quinoa, a recipe that varies from region to region (and cook to cook), but is usually composed of a thick, soupy base of quinoa, potatoes, tubers, squash, and any other vegetables that might be on hand.

MAKES 6 CUPS / 4 SERVINGS

1 Tbsp coconut oil

½ large white onion, diced

1 medium carrot, finely chopped

1 stalk celery, finely chopped

3 cloves garlic, minced

¾ lb purple, red, and/or yellow baby potatoes, cut into ½-inch dice (about 2 cups)

½ cup quinoa

½ tsp dried oregano

½ tsp dried thyme

¼ tsp ground turmeric

½ tsp ground black pepper

½ lbs butternut squash, peeled and cut into ½-inch dice (about 2 cups)

4 cups Vegetable Broth (page 60, or store bought)

Sea salt

1 avocado, chopped

¼ cup chopped fresh cilantro

Warm the oil in a heavy-bottomed pot over medium heat. Add the onion, carrot, celery, and garlic, and cook for 5 minutes, stirring occasionally. Add the potatoes and stir constantly while cooking for 2–3 minutes longer. Stir in the quinoa, oregano, thyme, turmeric, and ground black pepper, then add the butternut squash and broth. If your broth is an unsalted (or low-salt) variety, add a couple of pinches of salt; if your broth is already salted, wait until the end of cooking to season as needed. Turn the heat to high and bring the mixture to a boil, cover the pot, and then reduce the heat to medium-low and simmer for 20 minutes. Uncover the pot and simmer the mixture for 5 minutes longer, using a spoon to partially mash the butternut squash to make a thicker, stew-like broth. Remove the pot from the heat, cover it once more, and let it stand for 10 minutes to allow the flavors to fully meld. Taste for seasoning, and add additional salt as needed, as well as a little water if a thinner stew is preferred. Serve the stew garnished with chopped avocado and cilantro.

SUPERFOOD BOOST: Add 2 cups of chopped, dark leafy greens—like kale or Swiss chard—to the pot in the last couple of minutes of cooking.

BLACK LENTIL & ARUGULA SOUP

One of my secrets to making extra-great lentils is to simmer them in mushroom broth instead of water—a practice that gives lentils an irresistibly earthy and almost meaty flavor. In this recipe, the same technique is used to great effect, and, compounded with the delicious flavor of celeriac (celery root), the soup gains rich tones of celery and potato. To achieve the ideal texture, be diligent about dicing the vegetables nice and small.

MAKES ABOUT 6 CUPS / 4 SERVINGS

2 Tbsp olive oil

1 yellow onion, diced small

1 carrot, cut into ¼-inch dice

1½ cups celeriac, peeled and cut into ¼-inch dice

2 cloves garlic, minced

Sea salt and ground black pepper

1 cup black lentils

1 bay leaf

8 cups Mushroom Broth (page 62, or store bought)

2 Tbsp lemon juice

3 cups arugula

¼ cup chopped flat-leaf parsley

In a heavy-bottomed pot, heat the olive oil over medium heat. Add the onion and carrot, and cook until slightly softened, about 3–4 minutes. Add the celeriac, garlic, and a pinch of salt, and cook for 3–4 minutes longer, or until the celery root begins to turn golden. Add the lentils, bay leaf, and broth. Bring to a boil over high heat, then reduce the heat to low and simmer for 20–25 minutes, or until the lentils are tender. Remove from the heat and stir in the lemon juice and arugula. Remove the bay leaf, then taste and adjust seasonings as desired. Serve warm, with chopped parsley scattered on top.

FEEL GOOD FACT: Aside from black lentils containing heart-healthy antioxidants, fiber, and iron, they also contain a tremendous amount of protein: impressively, the one cup called for in this recipe contains more protein than eight eggs!

QUINOA RATATOUILLE STEW

Leave it to Alice Walters, Queen of All Things Natural and Wonderfully Simple, to devise a method of preparing ratatouille that reduces the notorious complexity of this classic recipe by slashing the number of steps. I use the same progression for my stew-y version, which celebrates the juiciness of warm-weather veggies, along with softened goji berries and toothsome quinoa. This stew gets better the longer it sits, so if you can muster a little patience, make it an hour or two before serving.

MAKES ABOUT 6 CUPS / 4 SERVINGS

½ large eggplant, cut into ½-inch dice

Sea salt and ground black pepper

2 Tbsp olive oil, divided, plus more for garnish

1 medium yellow onion, finely diced

3 cloves garlic, minced

1 medium red bell pepper, cut into ½-inch dice

1 small zucchini, cut into ½-inch dice

1 small yellow squash, cut into ½-inch dice

2 medium tomatoes, cut into ½-inch dice

3 Tbsp dried goji berries

½ cup fresh basil, chopped, plus more for garnish

3 cups Miso Broth (page 63, or store bought)

1 cup cooked quinoa

1 Tbsp red wine vinegar

Place the eggplant in a bowl and toss with ½ teaspoon sea salt. Set aside for 30 minutes. Remove the eggplant from the bowl and pat dry to remove excess moisture.

In a heavy-bottomed pot, warm 1 tablespoon of the olive oil over moderate heat. Add the eggplant and cook, stirring often, for 7 minutes to soften. Transfer the eggplant to a bowl.

In the same pot over moderate heat, add the remaining 1 tablespoon of olive oil. Add the onion, season with ¼ teaspoon sea salt and a little ground black pepper, and cook until the onion is softened and translucent, about 5 minutes. Add the garlic and cook for 1 minute longer. Stir in the bell pepper and cook for about 3–4 minutes. Add the zucchini and yellow squash and cook for 3–4 minutes longer. Add the tomatoes and cook for 10 minutes to break them down, stirring often. Toss in the goji berries and basil, and cook, stirring, for 1 minute. Add the broth, cooked quinoa, and reserved eggplant. Bring the mixture to a simmer and cook it on low heat for 10 minutes. Remove the pot from the heat, mix in the red wine vinegar, and adjust seasoning with salt if desired. Serve the stew, either warm or cold, drizzled lightly with olive oil and sprinkled with additional chopped fresh basil.

RED BEAN BORSCHT

Red kidney beans do a great job of making this classic Central and Eastern European soup extra hearty, and a generous addition of dulse adds a welcome bit of briny flavor and additional minerals. While you can get away with topping this borscht with a creamy garnish other than Horseradish Cream (unsweetened coconut yogurt, for example), don't skip the dill—it elevates and balances the deep rooty flavor of the beets.

MAKES 8 CUPS / 4 SERVINGS

1 Tbsp coconut oil

1 medium sweet yellow onion, finely diced

2 small carrots, cut into thin rounds

1 Tbsp tomato paste

½ medium celeriac (celery root), peeled and cut into ¼-inch dice (about 1 cup)

1 large Yukon gold potato, peeled and cut into ¼-inch dice (about 2 cups)

1 lb beets, peeled and cut into ¼-inch dice

2 Tbsp dulse flakes

3 cups Vegetable Broth (page 60, or store bought)

3 cups water

Sea salt and ground black pepper

2 cups cooked red kidney beans (page 13, or 1 15-oz can, drained)

1 large tart green apple, peeled and shredded

2 Tbsp red wine vinegar, or to taste

½ cup Horseradish Cream (page 202)

¼ cup fresh dill, chopped

Heat the oil in a large heavy-bottomed pot over medium heat. Add the onion and carrots, and stir often until softened, about 8–10 minutes. Add the tomato paste and cook for 1 minute longer, stirring constantly. Add the celeriac, potato, beets, dulse, broth, water, ¼ teaspoon sea salt, and ¼ teaspoon ground black pepper. Bring the mixture to a boil, and then reduce the heat to a low simmer. Cover the pot and cook the mixture for 20 minutes. Stir in the kidney beans and apple and cook covered for 10 minutes longer, or until the vegetables are tender, adding additional water if needed. Remove the pot from the heat and add the vinegar. Taste for seasoning, adding more salt, pepper, and vinegar, if needed. Serve the borscht warm, topped with a dollop of Horseradish Cream, and scattered with dill.

BLACK-EYED PEA JAMBALAYA

Like most families, mine has its share of strange traditions. Making jambalaya with my dad around the New Year is one of them. While neither of us can recall why this tradition began, we never miss a chance to enjoy this flavorful favorite together, which seems to get better every year.

MAKES 12 CUPS / 10 SERVINGS

2 Tbsp coconut oil

½ yellow onion, finely chopped

2 stalks celery, finely chopped

1 green bell pepper, seeded and cut into ½-inch dice

4 cloves garlic, minced

16 oz tempeh, cut into ½-inch dice

2 cups seeded and chopped tomatoes

¼ cup minced fresh parsley, plus additional for garnish

1 Tbsp fresh thyme, minced

Sea salt and ground black pepper

1 lb dry black-eyed peas

1 cup sorghum

4 bay leaves

3 Tbsp dulse flakes

1 Tbsp ground paprika

1 tsp dried oregano

¼ tsp cayenne powder

10 cups Miso Broth (page 63, or store bought)

¼ tsp liquid smoke

½ cup green onions, white and light green parts chopped, plus additional for garnish

Warm the coconut oil in a heavy-bottomed pot over medium heat. Add the onion, celery, bell pepper, and garlic, and cook for 5 minutes to soften. Stir in the tempeh and cook for 5–6 minutes longer, until the tempeh begins to turn golden. Add the tomatoes, parsley, thyme, and ¼ teaspoon salt and cook 5–6 minutes longer. Add the black-eyed peas, sorghum, bay leaves, dulse flakes, paprika, oregano, cayenne, and 1 teaspoon ground black pepper. Pour in the broth and liquid smoke, stirring to combine. Turn the heat to high and bring the mixture to a boil. Cover the pot, reduce the heat to medium-low, and simmer for 1 hour.

Remove the pot cover and stir in the green onions. Simmer, uncovered, for 15 minutes. Remove the pot from the heat, and let the jambalaya stand for a minimum of 15 minutes longer. Taste, and adjust seasoning if desired. To serve, remove the bay leaves and ladle the jambalaya into serving bowls, topping each with some of the green onions and parsley, as desired.

Optional: *Add a couple shakes of your favorite hot sauce for additional heat.*

WHITE BEAN & WINTER SQUASH
SOUP WITH KALE

You can use just about any variety of hard winter squash in this recipe, from butternut to kabocha (my current favorite is blue hubbard squash, which is so good I've vowed to put it in my garden next year). This great weeknight soup comes together in less than half an hour, and it is packed with protein, fiber, and minerals for an easy, balanced meal.

MAKES 8 CUPS / 4 SERVINGS

1 Tbsp olive oil

1 large sweet onion, finely diced

4 garlic cloves, minced

1 tsp fresh rosemary, minced

1 lb winter squash, such as hubbard or kabocha, peeled and cut into ½-inch dice (3 cups)

3 cups cooked cannellini beans (page 13, or 2 15-oz cans, drained)

4 cups Miso Broth (page 63, or store bought)

Sea salt and ground black pepper

2 tsp white wine vinegar

5 cups (packed) baby kale

3 Tbsp tahini, divided

⅓ cup hemp seeds, divided

¼ cup micro greens, for serving (optional)

Warm the oil in a large heavy-bottomed pot over medium heat. Add the onion and cook until translucent, about 5 minutes. Stir in the garlic and rosemary, and cook for 1 minute longer. Add the winter squash, beans, and broth, along with ½ teaspoon sea salt and ½ teaspoon ground black pepper. On high heat, bring the mixture to a boil, and then reduce the heat to low, cover the pot, and simmer for 15 minutes, or until the squash is very soft. Remove the pot from the heat and use the back of a soup spoon to mash some of the squash into the broth until the soup has slightly thickened. Stir in the vinegar, baby kale, 1 tablespoon of the tahini, and 2 tablespoons of the hemp seeds. Cover the pot and let the soup rest for 5 minutes, then taste and adjust seasonings, if desired. Ladle the soup into serving bowls and lightly drizzle each with the remaining tahini. Generously scatter the remaining hemp seeds on top of each bowl and crown with a small bundle of micro greens.

FEEL GOOD FACT: Hemp seeds are a wonderful beauty food, full of omega 3 fats and vitamin E, two nutrients which are well known to promote shiny hair, strong nails, and radiant skin.

POZOLE VERDE WITH PINTO BEANS

It's hard to live in Southern California and not be influenced by (read: addicted to) seriously great Mexican cuisine. Such is the case with my obsession with pozole—a popular Mexican stew made with hominy (puffy maize kernels that taste like a freshly made corn tortilla). This green, plant-based (and protein-rich) version of pozole is downright heroic for lovers of "loud" food, with its bold corn flavor, fun chewy texture, and generous pepper, herb, and lime seasonings. You can find dried or canned hominy in most supermarkets where other ingredients for Mexican food are shelved.

MAKES 8 CUPS / 4–6 SERVINGS

1 large white onion, peeled, trimmed, and quartered

2 cloves garlic, smashed with peel

2 poblano peppers

1 jalapeño pepper

2 stalks celery, quartered

2 Tbsp yellow miso paste

1 cup packed cilantro, divided, plus extra for garnish

8 cups water, divided

1 Tbsp olive oil

½ cup amaranth

3 cups cooked hominy (freshly cooked or 1 28-oz can, drained)

1½ cups cooked pinto beans (page 13, or 1 15-oz can, drained)

2 tsp dried oregano

Sea salt

¼ cup fresh lime juice

¼ cup Cashew Sour Cream (page 210, or store bought)

1 large avocado, diced

4 radishes (any variety), sliced paper-thin

Warm a heavy-bottomed pot over medium heat. Place the onion pieces cut side down inside, along with the unpeeled garlic, whole poblanos, jalapeño, and celery. Dry roast for 10 minutes to char, turning the vegetables every few minutes—take the garlic out after about 5 minutes, and remove the peel. Once charred, transfer the onion, celery, and garlic to a blender. When the peppers are cool enough to handle, trim the tops, remove all of the seeds, and add to the blender as well. Add the miso paste, ¾ cup of the cilantro, and 4 cups of water. Blend until smooth.

In the same pot, add the olive oil and warm it over medium heat. Pour in the blended mixture, and cook for 5 minutes, stirring, to reduce slightly. Add the amaranth, hominy, pinto beans, oregano, and ½ teaspoon sea salt, and pour in the remaining 4 cups water. Bring the mixture to a boil over high heat, then reduce the heat to medium and simmer for 20 minutes.

Remove the pot from the heat, and stir in the lime juice and remaining ¼ cup cilantro. Let the soup rest for 5 minutes, and then adjust seasoning to taste. To serve, divide into bowls, and top each with a dollop of Cashew Sour Cream, avocado chunks, sliced radish, and a few cilantro leaves for garnish.

FRITZ'S (DOGGY) SUPERFOOD STEW

At 90 pounds, my German shepherd, Fritz, is clearly not one to pass up a meal. But after an intensive dental procedure, he was put under strict doctor's orders to eat only soft foods for a few days. This stew was my solution to help him heal quickly and restore his energy. It's full of restorative protein, anti-inflammatory fats, important minerals (like calcium), and antioxidant-rich greens—a combo that he fell in love with so exuberantly that I still mix it into some of his dry food from time to time. The stew is incredibly easy to prepare and highly flexible, in terms of ingredients, and it always makes me feel good that Fritz is getting REAL, awesome food.

Note: *Serving size will vary, based on your own four-legged buddy. If you have a highly picky appetite to feed, try adding a spoonful of salt-free/sugar-free peanut butter to the blend.*

MAKES 8 CUPS

1½ cups yams and/or carrots, cut into 1-inch dice

¾ cup long-grain brown rice

1 cup lentils (any variety)

2 Tbsp kelp powder or other dry seaweed

8 cups water, plus more as needed

1 cup finely chopped broccoli or kale

⅓ cup hemp seeds

2 Tbsp flax oil (optional)

Additional superfood boosts (see next page)

In a heavy-bottomed pot, combine the yams and/or carrots, rice, lentils, kelp powder, and water. Bring the mixture to a boil over high heat, then cover the pot and reduce the heat to medium-low. Simmer the mixture for 45 minutes. Remove the cover, add the broccoli and hemp seeds, and cook until the broccoli is tender, about 5–10 minutes longer. Remove the pot from the heat and stir in the flax oil. Let the stew cool to room temperature before serving, and add any additional superfood boosts as desired, and extra water, if needed. The stew may be served as is, with extra water on the side, and along with other foods. It will last up to 1 week in the refrigerator.

Never give your dog: *Cacao, chocolate, raisins, grapes, avocado, onions, garlic, walnuts, macadamia nuts, extra salt, or extra sugar.*

SUPERFOOD BOOSTS

You can add many other superfoods to your doggy stew, including:

* MEDICINAL MUSHROOMS, such as a handful of chopped shiitake, or a spoonful of cordyceps, for energy. (Cook the mushrooms with the soup.)

* A HANDFUL OF CHIA SEEDS for skin, joint, and bone health. (Mix in the chia when the stew has cooled.)

* A SPRINKLE OF SPIRULINA for an immunity boost and to promote a fresher smell for your dog. (Mix in the spirulina when the stew has cooled.)

* A SPRINKLE OF WHEATGRASS to help digestion and blood flow. (Mix in the wheatgrass when the stew has cooled.)

* MINCED FRESH PARSLEY OR KALE for good breath and detoxification. (Add at any time.)

* A SMALL HANDFUL OF GOJI BERRIES for beta-carotene and anti-cancer protection. (Cook the goji berries with the stew.)

SOUP ACCOUTREMENTS

Presentation matters, and not just because we eat with our eyes. When you accessorize soups with special garnishes, seasoning mixes, nut creams, chutneys, seeds, and so on, you are adding layers of flavor and texture that take recipes to new heights and enhance the sensory appeal, so you can enjoy soups on a more holistic level. To that end, you'll find several options for soup accoutrements in this chapter (most of which offer additional superfood benefits), from fiery harissas to truly addictive Coconut Bacon Bits (page 209).

� = FEATURED SUPERFOOD INGREDIENT

✻ BEAUTY   ◉ BONE STRENGTH   🍃 CLEANSE/DETOX

♥ HEART HEALTH   ✺ IMMUNITY   ◊ LOW CALORIE   ⬡ PROTEIN

SUPER SIMPLE SOUP GARNISHES

Soup toppings can be as complex or as simple as you like. In addition to the enticing recipes in this chapter, here are a few extra-simple ingredients you can use to healthfully boost the aesthetic appeal and flavor of your soups:

* Chopped hazelnuts, pistachios, and almonds
* Hemp seeds, chia seeds, and pumpkin seeds
* A light drizzle of yacon syrup, or other syrup of your choice
* A light drizzle of flavorful oil, such as olive or hemp oil, or oils blended with herbs or superfood powders
* Coconut milk (canned) or a blended cashew cream
* Chopped, dried, semisweet fruit, like goji berries and goldenberries
* Sprouts and microgreens
* Chopped fresh herbs, like parsley, cilantro, and basil

* Sliced green onions (scallions) and chives
* A light dusting of a mild complementary spice, like turmeric, chili powder, or black pepper
* A light dusting of a mild superfood powder, like chaga or cacao powder
* Pretty produce, such as a couple of baby beet leaves, shaved radish, or minced bell pepper
* Edible flower petals
* Crispy, low-sugar, whole-grain cereals
* Popcorn
* Croutons

HOW TO MAKE BAKED TORTILLA CHIPS

Why buy 'em when you can bake 'em?

6 6-inch corn tortillas

1 Tbsp neutral-flavored oil, such as grapeseed oil

Sea salt, to taste

Preheat the oven to 350°F. Spray two baking sheets with cooking spray.

One at a time, lightly brush both sides of each tortilla with oil. Stack the tortillas together, and cut them into six wedges. Place them on the baking sheets in a single layer. Sprinkle the wedges with salt. Bake the tortillas for 8–15 minutes, rotating the pans halfway through cooking, or until they're golden brown and crisp. Chips burn easily, so keep an eye on them toward the end of cooking (remove any cooked chips and return the tray to the oven). When all the chips are done, remove the tray from the oven and allow the chips to cool for several minutes (they'll continue to crisp as they cool).

HORSERADISH CREAM

Don't be fooled by the simplicity of this recipe—it really makes a soup pop! Try it with potato-based, hearty mushroom and grain, or traditional beet soups.

MAKES ABOUT ⅔ CUP

⅓ cup raw cashews

⅓ cup filtered water

1 Tbsp prepared horseradish

½ tsp apple cider vinegar

1 tsp camu powder

In a mini blender, blend all of the ingredients until they are smooth. Refrigerate the mixture until you're ready to use. It will keep for up to 2 weeks.

HOW TO MAKE ZA'ATAR

Za'atar is a spice blend that is attributed to Middle Eastern culinary culture. Although there's no single recipe for the blend, it's usually composed of a mix of toasted sesame seeds, sumac, fresh or dried green herbs (such as thyme, marjoram, mint, and oregano), salt, and other spices (such as ground cumin or coriander). Za'atar can be used as a topping for all kinds of soups, and will last for several weeks at room temperature, or a couple of months in the refrigerator.

MAKES ⅓ CUP

1 Tbsp dried oregano

1 Tbsp dried thyme

2 Tbsp ground sumac

1 Tbsp toasted sesame seeds

1 tsp sea salt

Combine all ingredients in a spice grinder, and briefly blitz into a coarse powder. Store in a sealed container in the refrigerator for maximum shelf life.

CHIA PESTO

The bulky quality of chia seed "gel" (chia seeds that have been soaked in liquid) is a fabulous way of shaving off calories and upping the nutrient density in pesto, compared to the classic recipe. Aside from being outstanding in grain or squash soups, this special sauce can also be used for all kinds of pasta and roasted vegetable dishes.

MAKES 1 CUP

1 Tbsp chia seeds

6 Tbsp water or vegetable broth

1 cup (packed) fresh basil leaves

3 Tbsp pine nuts

1 large clove garlic, thinly sliced

¼ cup olive oil

¼ cup nutritional yeast

½ tsp sea salt

In a medium bowl, mix together the chia seeds and water or broth. Set aside for 10 minutes to allow the chia seeds to swell, stirring once or twice to break up any clumps.

In a food processor, combine the basil, pine nuts, garlic, olive oil, nutritional yeast, and salt. Blend until smooth. Scrape the pesto into the bowl with the chia seeds, and mix well to incorporate. Cover, and refrigerate until ready to use. Chia pesto will last up to 1 week, refrigerated.

FEEL GOOD FACT: Chia seeds are an amazing food for bone strength. Offering 5-6 times more calcium than milk, gram for gram, just a single tablespoon of chia seeds provides 14% of your daily calcium needs.

GREEN HARISSA

Harissa is usually prepared with red chilis (like the superfood version on page 206), but green harissa, which is made with an abundance of fresh herbs, has found its way onto restaurant menus in the past several years. You can use this bright green sauce to liven up almost any kind of soup—it's especially good in recipes that are tomato-, root-, or tuber-based, as well as hearty bean stews. But really, just put it on everything.

MAKES ¾ CUP

1 Tbsp cumin seeds

1 Tbsp coriander seeds

2 jalapeño peppers, seeded and sliced thin, with seeds reserved

1 cup (packed) cilantro leaves and stems

½ cup (packed) flat leaf parsley

1 small clove garlic, smashed

1½ tsp wheatgrass powder (optional)

2 Tbsp fresh lime juice

⅓ cup olive oil, plus extra for storage

¾ tsp sea salt

Heat a small skillet over medium-high heat. Add the cumin and coriander seeds and cook until fragrant, about 2–3 minutes, then let cool. Place the spices and all the remaining ingredients, except the reserved jalapeño seeds, in a food processor and blend into a smooth sauce. Taste, and blend in a few jalapeño seeds if more heat is desired.

Refrigerate the harissa in a small covered container with a little olive oil poured on top to keep it from oxygenating and turning brown. Green Harissa will last for up to 2 weeks in the refrigerator.

SUPERFOOD TIP: To minimize green color loss through oxygenation without adding extra oil, simply press a piece of plastic wrap directly onto the surface of the harissa before refrigerating.

GOJI HARISSA

Although the traditional recipe for this North African chili sauce does not include goji berries, they enhance the blend with a mild, smoky sweetness and add fruity notes to the chiles. Many kinds of chiles will do great in this recipe: you can usually find large dried red chiles in the international foods section of your local market. Just be aware that the heat levels of chiles vary dramatically (Guajillo and New Mexico chiles, as used in the recipe below, are known to be mild). Goji Harissa can be used in potato or squash-based soups, fruit soups (like mango or melon), tomato soups, and more.

MAKES ¾ CUP

6 large dried Guajillo or
New Mexico chiles

¼ cup dried goji berries

½ tsp caraway seeds

¼ tsp cumin seeds

¼ tsp coriander seeds

2 tsp ground paprika

¼ tsp chipotle powder

¼ tsp cayenne pepper

2 cloves garlic, crushed

1 tsp sea salt

2 Tbsp fresh lemon juice

⅓ cup olive oil

Place the chiles in a large heatproof bowl and cover with boiling water. Let the chiles soak for 20 minutes, covered, and then add the goji berries and soak until the goji berries are soft and saturated, about 5–10 minutes longer. Drain away the liquid. Snip off the ends of the chiles and drain out the seeds.

Combine the caraway, cumin, and coriander seeds in a small skillet over medium-high heat. Toast the seeds until they are fragrant and slightly golden, about 2–3 minutes. Use a mortar and pestle or spice grinder to crush the spices. Place the ground spices in a food processor, and add the chiles and goji berries, as well as all the remaining ingredients. Purée the mixture, stopping the machine and scraping down the sides as needed, until a smooth paste has formed (this may take a couple of minutes). Transfer to a sealable jar, and refrigerate until ready to use. Goji Harissa will last up to 2 weeks in the refrigerator.

SUPERFOOD BOOST: For a blast of extra vitamin C, add ½ teaspoon camu powder when adding the ground spices to the food processor.

COCONUT BACON BITS

When the news broke recently that eating processed meats like bacon definitively increases the risk of cancer, Time *magazine responded with a cover story titled "The War on Delicious." This recipe for Coconut Bacon Bits begs to differ! With a balance of crunchy and chewy, and loads of mouth-watering bacon-like flavor, you can feel great about eating these savory bits, because they are composed of heart-healthy coconut and antioxidant-rich spices. Go ahead and sprinkle them on just about any of your favorite recipes: they are particularly delicious on creamy chowders, chilis, and potato-based soups. And while you may not think you'll need the full 1½ cups that the recipe yields, trust me when I say that once you taste these bacon-y coconut bits, you'll have plenty motivation to use them again and again.*

MAKES 1½ CUPS

2 Tbsp tamari

1 Tbsp maple syrup

½ tsp hickory liquid smoke

½ tsp smoked paprika

½ tsp onion powder

½ tsp chipotle powder

1 tsp ground sumac

½ tsp sea salt

½ tsp ground black pepper

1 Tbsp coconut oil

1½ cups coconut flakes

Line a large plate with a paper towel and set aside.

In a small bowl, whisk together the tamari, maple syrup, liquid smoke, paprika, onion powder, chipotle powder, ground sumac, sea salt, and black pepper. Place the bowl in easy reach of the stove.

Warm the coconut oil in a large skillet over medium heat. Test the oil to make sure it's piping hot by adding a single coconut flake—if it sizzles, the pan is ready. If it doesn't sizzle, wait another minute, or until the coconut flake begins to bubble and hiss. Once the oil is hot, add the coconut flakes to the pan. Stirring constantly, so as not to burn them, toast the coconut flakes until they are golden brown, about 2–3 minutes. Add the tamari-spice mixture and stir continually for 1 minute longer to allow the extra moisture to dissipate. Immediately transfer the coconut to the prepared plate, spreading the toasted flakes over the surface of the towel to absorb excess oil. Let the coconut bits sit for 20 minutes to cool and slightly crisp. Store them at room temperature in a sealed container, where they will keep for about 1 month.

CASHEW SOUR CREAM

While there may be no bona fide superfoods in this recipe, I would be remiss to send you into the world of superfood soups without a way to embellish your recipes with a healthier spin on sour cream. A dollop of this delightful cashew-based cream—which is cholesterol-free and rich in protein, minerals, and skin-healthy fats—is sensational on chilis and hearty grain soups, and only gets better the longer it sits in your fridge.

MAKES 1¾ CUPS

1 cup raw cashews, soaked in water 4–6 hours or overnight

⅔ cup water

¼ cup apple cider vinegar

2 Tbsp yellow miso paste

1 tsp sunflower lecithin (optional)*

3 Tbsp coconut oil

Drain and rinse the cashews. Place them in a food processor and add all the remaining ingredients except the coconut oil. Process the mixture for several minutes, stopping the machine and scraping down the sides, as needed, until a smooth whip has formed. Add the coconut oil, and process until it is fully incorporated. Transfer the mixture to a sealable container. Cover the container and refrigerate for a minimum of 1 hour (ideally overnight) to let it firm up before serving. Cashew Sour Cream will keep for up to 2 weeks in the refrigerator—and the flavor will only improve with age.

* Lecithin will not change the flavor of this recipe, but it will help make it extra silky. You may also use soy lecithin instead of sunflower lecithin, or omit it altogether.

FEEL GOOD FACT: Cashews are a great source of many minerals, in particular, iron and magnesium. In fact, a single one-ounce serving of cashews has 20% of your daily magnesium, which is why this nut is so revered for its support of bone health and heart health.

CANDIED SEED CLUSTERS

Seeds are a wonderful way to add a delightfully soft crunch to soup, along with copious minerals, good fats, and extra protein. These lightly spiced, candied clusters taste the best atop root or squash soups, as well as chilis and spicy stews. You can easily make variations on this recipe by using additional sweet spices, such as cinnamon and cloves, or savory ones, such as sage and rosemary.

MAKES 2 CUPS

¼ cup hemp seeds

1 Tbsp black sesame seeds

1 Tbsp chia seeds

2 Tbsp coconut sugar

½ tsp ground nutmeg

⅛ tsp cayenne pepper

½ tsp ground black pepper

¼ tsp sea salt

2 Tbsp maple syrup

½ cup raw sunflower seeds

2 Tbsp raw pumpkin seeds (pepitas)

Mix together the hemp seeds, sesame seeds, chia seeds, coconut sugar, nutmeg, cayenne, black pepper, and sea salt. Mix in the maple syrup until it is well incorporated, and set aside.

Warm a small skillet over medium heat. Add the sunflower seeds and pepitas and cook for 3–4 minutes, stirring often, until the pepitas slightly swell. Add the maple syrup–coated seeds to the sunflower and pepita mix, stirring constantly, and cook for about 1 minute longer. Transfer the mixture to a plate to cool and harden, about 10 minutes, then break it into small pieces. Candied Seed Clusters will keep for a couple of months, stored in an airtight container, at room temperature.

GOLDENBERRY CHUTNEY

This citrusy, savory spread can be used in a couple of exciting ways—to lighten up puréed soups, especially root soups, or as a spread for toasted bread (perfect to serve alongside a bowl of warm stew). No matter how you use it, Goldenberry Chutney is a great secret weapon to have in the refrigerator.

MAKES ⅔ CUP

12 small pearl onions, peeled

½ cup dried goldenberries

⅛ tsp allspice

1 Tbsp coconut sugar

1 cup Vegetable Broth (page 60, or store bought)

Pinch saffron (optional)

Combine all the ingredients in a small pot over medium heat. Bring to a boil, then reduce the heat and cook for 25–30 minutes until the onions are translucent and the liquid is reduced to syrup. Transfer to a food processor and process into a chunky paste. Goldenberry Chutney will last for several weeks, refrigerated in a sealed container.

APPLE SLAW

A super-fresh topping for both warm and cold soups.

1 crispy apple (such as Fuji), minced

2 Tbsp minced fresh parsley

½ Tbsp olive oil

½ tsp Dijon mustard

1 tsp apple cider vinegar

Sea salt and ground black pepper to taste

Combine all the ingredients in a mixing bowl and toss, seasoning with salt and pepper to taste. Refrigerate until ready to use.

HEMP SEED PARMESAN

The first restaurant I worked in was Italian, a place that was well known in the community for two things: a garlicky bread dip that was worth buying by the bucket, and fragrant boulders of fresh Parmesan that were nestled in damp cloths and presented for table-side grating. I finally created a superfood version that's parmesan-like and is refrigerated as a chunk, ready to be freshly grated, sliced, or crumbled—it even slightly melts. Hemp Seed Parmesan keeps for several weeks in the refrigerator, and it is probably one of the soup toppings I use the most.

MAKES 8 OUNCES

⅔ cup raw cashews
⅓ cup hemp seeds
2 Tbsp nutritional yeast
¼ tsp sea salt
2 Tbsp white miso paste
1 Tbsp coconut oil

Add the cashews to a food processor and grind into a powder. Add the hemp seeds, nutritional yeast, sea salt, miso paste, and coconut oil, and process briefly into a paste.

Place the paste on top of a sheet of parchment paper. Mold the paste into a loose brick, wrap it tightly in the paper, and wrap again with plastic. Freeze the paste for 2 hours, or until it is firm, then move it to the refrigerator to store.

To serve the Hemp Seed Parmesan, use a cheese grater, shaver, or a thin knife to slice it into thin pieces and use as a topping for soups of all varieties that might do well with a cheesy topping. Hemp Seed Parmesan softens easily, so keep it in the refrigerator, wrapped in parchment paper and stored in a sealable container or plastic for long-term storage. It will last for about 1 month.

SUPERFOOD TIP: If you can't stand the wait, and need a Parmesan-style topping in a pinch, here's an (almost) instant fix: blitz together ¼ cup hemp seeds, 1 tablespoon nutritional yeast, and ¼ teaspoon sea salt in a food processor, and sprinkle away!

SPROUTED CROUTONS

♥

Most days, I reach for some crunchy seeds, chopped nuts, or minced herbs to adorn my soup du jour. But sometimes—and we've all been there—only a crispy fresh crouton will do. To keep things easy, I make mine at home from the same bread we use for our morning toast. It's made from sprouted grains, which means more protein, more micronutrients, and easier digestibility. (Many delicious varieties of sprouted breads are now available in most grocery stores, but if you can't find a sprouted variety, any bread will do.) A little bit of chia gives this extra-basic recipe a simple superfood upgrade.

MAKES 2 CUPS

4 slices sprouted grain bread*

2 Tbsp olive oil

1 Tbsp chia seeds

¼ tsp sea salt

*gluten-free bread may also be used

Preheat the oven to 350°F.

Tear the bread into bite-size pieces (or loosely a ¾-inch square) over a large bowl. Drizzle with olive oil and sprinkle with chia seeds and salt. Toss by hand to evenly distribute the ingredients and spread them on a large baking sheet. Use a few of the croutons to swipe any remaining chia seeds from the bowl onto the pan. Bake the croutons for 15–20 minutes, or until they are well toasted.

Croutons may be stored at room temperature for several days, and recrisped in a warm oven as needed.

Variation: *Add herbs and spices to create new flavors! Try mixing in a clove of minced garlic, a few pinches of freshly chopped thyme, or even some nutritional yeast and onion powder for a cheesy variation.*

BEYOND BREAD

There's no denying that bread and soup are a great combo—and I am the first to admit that I sometimes indulge in a warm crusty loaf. What could be more delicious than saddling a freshly made bowl of soup with a slice of toasted bread? Classic.

Deliciousness aside, the downside to bread is that unless it's sprouted, it's not particularly nutrient-dense. This translates into calories that don't have much of a positive impact, and you need to consume more of them to feel satisfyingly full. By no means am I trying to demonize bread (my goodness, there are far, far worse foods in the world)—it's just nice to have other options. So, to make your soup feel like a meal, maybe try one of these types of starches instead. Each offers a little more bang for your buck, nutritionally speaking.

Baked potato. This is basically nature's version of a bread bowl. Any kind of chili, stew, or even chowder is fantastic poured on top of a steaming baked potato, which, despite its humble reputation, actually provides a healthy array of phytonutrients that have even shown potential in lowering blood pressure.

Baked sweet potato/winter squash. Here's another fabulous option that offers carotene antioxidants and a more pronounced sweet flavor. Sweet tubers and squashes are especially great with chilis and bean soups.

Dark leafy greens. In my house, we call this "soup-on-salad style." Alas, it's not exactly the most glamorous dish you've ever laid eyes on. But, if I'm being totally honest, it is one of my favorite homestyle ways to enjoy soup: simply pack a large bowl with dark baby greens like spinach or kale, then pour hot soup on top. The greens wilt and add filling bulk, while the soup acts like a very heavy salad dressing. You can use virtually any kind of soup for these recipes; one of my favorites is lentil. Of course, you can always just serve a salad on the side and have an exceptionally satisfying (and much prettier!) healthy meal.

Cooked grains. Transform your soup into a loose pilaf by pouring it over a layer of cooked quinoa, freekeh, rice, or your grain of choice. (Why eat processed bread when you can just eat the whole grain as-is and gain *all* of its natural health benefits?)

Any combo of the above. If you layer a couple of the above options under your soup du jour, you'll create one of the world's best lunch or dinner bowls. Bread is no match for the feeling of satisfaction you'll gain from this medley of whole foods.

If you are a die-hard bread fan (I live with one—dear me, I understand!), try swapping your day-to-day bread with a loaf that is made from sprouted grains. This way, you'll get a much more protein- and mineral-rich bread that's also more filling and easier to digest. Remember, every better choice you make adds up and contributes to a healthier lifestyle overall.

PART THREE

EXTRAS

SUPERFOOD SUBSTITUTION CHEAT SHEET

Many superfoods can easily be swapped for each other, or even just a more commonplace food. So, if you can't get your hands on a particular ingredient, or have just run out, don't let that deter you from enjoying the recipes in this book! Though the nutrition of your soup will change, you'll still end up with a delicious bowlful.

Note: Substitutions can go both ways, and can be used in a 1:1 ratio.

SUPERFOOD		SUBSTITUTION
Amaranth (whole)	=	Quinoa (whole)
Cacao powder	=	Cocoa powder
Camu powder	=	Omit from recipe
Chia seeds	=	Flaxseeds for a topping; omit from recipe when in soup
Coconut sugar	=	Xylitol, date sugar, or cane sugar
Dates	=	Raisins
Farro	=	Spelt berries or sorghum
Freekeh	=	Cracked wheat or bulgur
Forbidden (black) rice	=	Brown rice
Hemp seeds	=	Sunflower seeds
Kale	=	Swiss chard, or other dark leafy green
Kelp	=	Pinch of sea salt, or omit from recipe
Maitake mushrooms (fresh)	=	Crimini mushrooms (fresh)
Mushroom powder (any variety)	=	Another powder (any variety), or omit from recipe
Quinoa flakes	=	Rolled oats
Shiitake mushrooms (fresh)	=	Crimini mushrooms (fresh)
Sorghum	=	Short-grain brown rice
Spirulina powder	=	Wheatgrass powder, or omit from recipe
Watercress	=	Arugula
Yacon slices (dried)	=	Apple slices (dried)
Yacon syrup	=	Maple syrup

CONVERSION CHART

NON-LIQUID INGREDIENTS (Weights of common ingredients in grams)

INGREDIENT	1 CUP	¾ CUP	⅔ CUP	½ CUP	⅓ CUP	¼ CUP	2 TBSP
Chia Seeds	163 g	122 g	108 g	81 g	54 g	41 g	20 g
Chopped fruits and vegetables	150 g	110 g	100 g	75 g	50 g	40 g	20 g
Dried goji berries/fruits	111 g	83 g	74 g	55 g	37 g	28 g	14 g
Nuts, chopped	150 g	110 g	100 g	75 g	50 g	40 g	20 g

Note: Non-liquid ingredients specified in American recipes by volume (if more than about 2 tablespoons or 1 fluid ounce) can be converted to weight with the table above. If you need to convert an ingredient that isn't in this table, the safest thing to do is to measure it with a traditional measuring cup and then weigh the results with a metric scale. In a pinch, you can use the volume conversion table below.

VOLUME CONVERSIONS
(USED FOR LIQUIDS)

CUSTOMARY QUANTITY	METRIC EQUIVALENT
1 teaspoon	5 mL
1 tablespoon or ½ fluid ounce	15 mL
¼ cup or 2 fluid ounces	60 mL
⅓ cup	80 mL
½ cup or 4 fluid ounces	120 mL
⅔ cup	160 mL
1 cup or 8 fluid ounces or ½ pint	250 mL
1½ cups or 12 fluid ounces	350 mL
2 cups or 1 pint or 16 fluid ounces	475 mL
3 cups or 1½ pints	700 mL

INGREDIENT RESOURCES GUIDE

NAVITAS NATURALS

Go-to source for sustainable, organic superfoods.

Find here: Cacao powder, camu powder, chia seeds, coconut sugar, dried goji berries, dried goldenberries, hemp seeds, maca powder, raw cashews, wheatgrass powder, yacon slices, and more.

Visit: navitasnaturals.com

OM—ORGANIC MUSHROOM NUTRITION

Specializes in organic medicinal mushroom powders and blends.

Find here: Chaga powder, cordyceps powder, reishi powder, and more.

Visit: ommushrooms.com

NUTREX-HAWAII

Best source for quality spirulina.

Find here: Spirulina powder.

Visit: nutrex-hawaii.com

MAINE COAST SEA VEGETABLES

Exceptional sustainably harvested and organic seaweeds.

Find here: Kelp granules, dulse flakes, nori sheets, and more.

Visit: seaveg.com

EDEN FOODS

A diverse natural and organic food line of specialty products—very useful resource for superfood soups.

Find here: Buckwheat noodles, BPA-free canned beans, kombu strips, ume vinegar, wakame flakes, and more.

Visit: edenfoods.com

LOTUS FOODS

Specializes in whole grain, heirloom, and specialty rice.

Find here: Black "forbidden" rice, rice ramen noodles.

Visit: lotusfoods.com

BOB'S RED MILL

Enormously vast line of dry pantry goods.

Find here: Amaranth, arrowroot powder, buckwheat groats, farro, freekeh, lentils, peas, quinoa, sorghum.

Visit: bobsredmill.com

MOUNTAIN ROSE HERBS

A good source for buying bulk organic herbs and spices.

Find here: A variety of culinary and medicinal herbs and spices, such as cinnamon and rose.

Visit: mountainroseherbs.com

AMAZON

The king of online shopping.

Find here: Almost any shelf-stable ingredient or kitchen supply you can't find in a store, such as spice grinders, pots, storage containers, and even specialty superfoods—often for a discounted price.

Visit: amazon.com

BIBLIOGRAPHY

American Society of Plant Biologists. "The Origin and spread of 'Emperor's rice.'" *Science Daily.* 26 September 2015. Web. 4 April 2016. https://www.sciencedaily.com/releases/2015/09/150926191819.htm.

Blaszyk, Amy. "Taking Stock of Bone Broth: Sorry, No Cure-All Here." *NPR.* 10 February 2015. Web. 4 April 2016. http://www.npr.org/sections/the-salt/2015/02/10/384948585/taking-stock-of-bone-broth-sorry-no-cure-all-here.

Bode, Ann M. and Zigang Dong. "The Amazing and Mighty Ginger." *Herbal Medicine: Biomolecular and Clinical Aspects. 2nd edition.* Web. 4 April 2016. http://www.ncbi.nlm.nih.gov/books/NBK92775/.

Callaway, J.C. "Hempseed as A Nutritional Resource: An Overview." *Euphytica.* 2004. Web. 7 April 2014. http://ovidsp.tx.ovid.com/sp-3.11.0a/ovidweb.cgi?T=JS&PAGE=fulltext&D=ovft&AN=00005768-201001000-00019&NEWS=N&CSC=Y&CHANNEL=PubMed.

Carbour, Celia and Rachel Mount. "25 Superfoods to Incorporate Into Your Diet Now." *Oprah.com.* Web. 4 April 2016. http://www.oprah.com/food/Superfoods-Ingredients-and-Recipes-for-a-Healthy-Diet.

Charles, Dan. "Heat, Drought Draw Farmers Back To Sorghum, The 'Camel Of Crops'." *NPR The Salt.* 31 October 2013. Web. 4 April 2016. http://www.npr.org/sections/the-salt/2013/10/31/231509864/heat-drought-draw-farmers-back-to-sorghum-the-camel-of-crops.

Clum, Dr. Lauren, and Dr. Mariza Snyder, *The Antioxidant Counter.* Berkley, CA: Ulysses Press, 2011.

Coates, Wayne, PhD. *Chia: The Complete Guide to the Ultimate Superfood.* New York, NY: Sterling, 2012.

Cooksley, Valerie Gennari. *Seaweed: Nature's Secret to Balancing Your Metabolism, Fighting Disease, and Revitalizing Body and Soul.* New York, NY: Stewart, Tabori and Chang, 2007.

Cornish, M. Lynn, et. al. "A role for dietary macroalgae in the amelioration of certain risk factors associated with cardiovascular disease." *International Pycological Society.* 54(6) (2015): 649-66. Web. 4 April 2016. http://www.phycologia.org/doi/pdf/10.2216/15-77.1.

Culinary Institute of America. *The Professional Chef.* New York, NY: John Wiley & Sons, Inc., 2002.

Dondero, Tim. "Dondero: Soups in ancient Rome." *Online Athens.* 18 April 2010. Web. 4 April 2016. http://onlineathens.com/stories/041810/liv_610999089.shtml#.VlYeUCR3heU.

"Effects of cooking on vitamins." *Beyond Vegetarianism.* Web. 4 April 2016. http://www.beyondveg.com/tu-j-l/raw-cooked/raw-cooked-2e.shtml.

"Goji Berry (Wolfberry)." *ImmuneHealthScience.com.* 2008-2013. Web. 8 April 2014. http://www.immunehealth-science.com/goji.html.

Halpern, Georges M. *Healing Mushrooms: Effective Treatments for Today's Illnesses.* New Hyde Park, NY: Square One, 2007.

Harrison-Dunn, Annie-Rose. "Add seaweed to food to improve heart health, Danish researchers urge industry." *Nutra Ingredients.* 25 November 2015. Web. 4 April 2016. http://www.nutraingredients.com/Research/Add-seaweed-to-food-to-improve-heart-health-Danish-researchers-urge-industry?nocount.

ISGA International Sprout Growers Association. Homepage. 17 Nov. 2014. http://www.isga-sprouts.org/.

Kazue, Noemia, et al. "Antibacterial activity of lentinula edodes grown in liquid medium." *Brazilian Journal of Microbiology.* 32(3) (Aug./Oct. 2001). Web. 4 April 2016. http://www.scielo.br/scielo.php?pid=S1517-83822001000300008&script=sci_arttext&tlng=pt.

Largeman-Roth, Frances. "Freekeh — The Next Hot Super-grain." *Huffpost Healthy Living*. 2 September 2013. Web. 4 April 2016. http://www.huffingtonpost.com/frances-largemanroth/best-supergrains_b_3824822.html.

Leech, Joe. "12 Proven Benefits of Pomegranate (No. 8 is Impressive)." *Authority Nutrition*. March 2016. Web. 4 April 2016. https://authoritynutrition.com/12-proven-benefits-of-pomegranate/.

Ley, Beth M., Ph.D. *Maca: Adaptogen and Hormonal Regulator*. Detroit Lakes, MN: BL Publications, 2003.

"Maca." Memorial Sloan-Kettering Cancer Center, April 2013. http://www.mskcc.org.

Maisto, Michelle. "Rediscovering Amaranth, The Aztec Superfood." *Forbes*. 5 Dec. 2011. Web. 17 Nov. 2014. http://www.forbes.com/sites/michellemaisto/2011/12/05/meet-amaranth-quinoas-ancient-superfood-cousin/.

Monro, JA, et al. "The risk of lead contamination in bone broth diets." *Medical Hypotheses*. 80(4) (April 2013): 389-90. Web. 9April 2014 http://www.ncbi.nlm.nih.gov/pubmed/23375414.

Morgan, Helen C., and Kelly J. Moorhead. *Spirulina: Nature's Superfood*. Nutrex Inc., 1993.

Rarback, Sheah. "Beyond broccoli: Green beans, radishes & radicchio are superstars." *Miami Herald*. 21 March 2016. Web. 4 April 2016. http://www.miamiherald.com/living/health-fitness/chew-on-this/article67393367.html.

Scholey, AB. "Cocoa polyphenols enhance positive mood states but not cognitive performance: a randomized, placebo-controlled trial." *International Journal of Biomedical Science*. 27(5) (May 2013): 451-8. Web. 9 April 2014. http://www.ncbi.nlm.nih.gov/pubmed/23364814.

Searby, Lyda. "Brown seaweed extract battles cancer." *Nutra Ingredients*. 30 November 2015. Web. 4 April 2016. http://www.nutraingredients.com/Research/Brown-seaweed-extract-battles-cancer.

"Soup and its history." *L'etoile Fine Virginia Cuisine*. 12 Jan 2011. Web. 4 April 2016. http://www.letoilerestaurant.com/history/soup-and-its-history/.

Sygo, Jennifer: "Jennifer Sygo: Introducing omega-7s, the new fatty acid on the block." *National Post*. 11 June 2013. Web. 4 April 2016. http://news.nationalpost.com/health/jennifer-sygo-introducing-omega-7s-the-new-fatty-acid-on-the-block.

Szalay, Jessie. "Potatoes: Health Benefits, Risks & Nutrition Facts." *Live Science*. 9 October 2014. Web. 4 April 2016. http://www.livescience.com/45838-potato-nutrition.html.

Weiss, Laura B. Farro: An Ancient and Complicated Grain Worth Figuring Out." *NPR Kitchen Window*. 2 October 2013. Web. 4 April 2016. http://www.npr.org/2013/10/02/227838385/farro-an-ancient-if-complicated-grain-worth-figuring-out.

Wolfe, David. *Chaga: King of the Medicinal Mushrooms*. Berkeley, California: North Atlantic Books, 2012.

Wong, Sam. "Scientists discover protein that boosts immunity to viruses and cancer." *Imperial College London*. 16 April 2015. Web. 4 April 2016. http://www3.imperial.ac.uk/newsandeventspggrp/imperialcollege/newssummary/news_16-4-2015-14-51-47

Young, Shelley Redford, and Robert O. Young. *The pH Miracle: Balance Your Diet, Reclaim Your Health*. Grand Central Life & Style, 2010.

Zeb, Alam. "Chemical and Nutritional Constituents of Sea Buckthorn Juice." *Pakistan Journal of Nutrition*. 3(2) (2004): 99-106. Web. 4 April 2016. http://www.pjbs.org/pjnonline/fin185.pdf.

Zielinski, Sarah. "Stone Age Stew? Soup Making May Be Older Than We'd Thought." NPR The Salt. 6 February 2013. Web. 4 April 2016. http://www.npr.org/sections/the-salt/2013/02/06/171104410/stone-age-stew-soup-making-may-be-older-than-wed-thought.

ACKNOWLEDGMENTS

Just as it takes many ingredients to make a good soup, so does it take a great team to create a book like this one. (And I think the pages within reflect what a joy it's been.)

Thank you to Oliver Barth for your many roles in this book: as a photographer, working with me side by side to create striking images; and as the most incredible partner, offering endless taste testing, support, love, and even dish-washing.

Thank you to my dad, for encouraging my occasional kitchen crashes and helping bring this book to life in our fun videos.

Thank you to my mom, for all your thoughtfulness, time, and sound writing suggestions. And thank you to Van Fleisher for your enthusiastic and detailed recipe testing.

Thank you to my agent Marilyn Allen for taking my seeded ideas and making sure they get planted and watered. I love the garden we have built.

Thank you to the entire publishing team at Sterling for all of your dedication and care to this project: To the coolest editor on the block, Jennifer Williams, for lending your impressive talents to fortify these pages; Christine Heun for the superb design; Elizabeth Lindy for the handsome cover art; Kimberly Broderick for navigating this whole ship; and major thank yous to Marilyn Kretzer, Theresa Thompson, Sari Lampert, Blanca Oliviery, Toula Ballas, Chris Vaccari, Victoria Horn, Sandra Ballabio, and Trudi Bartow for all of your incredible support and invested energies that bring this book out into the light! Big love to all of you.

Also thank you to Carolyn Pulvino for creating such flawless graphics. And thank you Alyssa Ochs for all your organizational contributions.

Thank you to my dear Navitas Naturals family for all the superfood support throughout this endeavor. And thank you to the team at Om Organic Mushroom Nutrition for sharing your knowledge and science.

Most of all, thank you to my beloved readers and fellow superfood devotees. It's your healthy actions and contagious enthusiasm that inspire me to always continue creating. Keep on shining.

SOUPS BY BENEFIT INDEX

For key to icons representing benefits,
see page 48.

✳ BEAUTY

◉ BONE STRENGTH

☙ CLEANSE/DETOX

LOW CALORIE

PROTEIN

INDEX

Note: Page numbers in *italics* indicate photos of recipes.

A

Accoutrements, 200–215
  about: bread alternatives, 215; garnishes, 201; making tortilla chips, 202; overview of, 200
  Apple Slaw, 212
  Candied Seed Clusters, 211
  Cashew Sour Cream, 210
  Chia Pesto, 204
  Coconut Bacon Bits, 208–209
  Goji Harissa, 206–207
  Goldenberry Chutney, 212
  Green Harissa, 205
  Hemp Seed Parmesan, 213
  Horseradish Cream, 202
  Sprouted Croutons, 214
  Za'atar (making), 203
Acid, for flat soup, 52
Acidity of foods, 47
Add-ins, 11, 15
African Minestrone Stew, 182
Algae
  about: boosting recipes with, 76, 153, 199; other recipe with, 81; resources for, 219; spirulina and chlorella, 25, 41; substitutions for, 217
  Spirulina Oil, 78
Alkalinity of foods, 47
Amaranth
  about: benefits and uses, 32, 33–34; cooking with, 40; resource for, 219; substitution for, 217
  Inca Chowder, 164
  Pozole Verde with Pinto Beans, 196–197
  Za'atar Amaranth Porridge, 169, 203
Apples
  Apple Slaw, 212
  Celeriac Soup with Applesauce & Watercress, 114
  Curried Apple and Butternut Squash Soup, 108–109
Aromatics, 8, 14
Artichoke Chowder, 158
Arugula
  about: benefits and uses, 24; other recipe with, 148; as watercress substitute, 217
  Black Lentil & Arugula Soup, 190
  Earl Grey Arugula Soup, 92
  Many Greens Soup, 106–107
  Za'atar Amaranth Porridge, 169, 203
Asparagus soup, truffled, 116–117
Avocados
  Avocado Nori Soup with Crispy Rice, 76

Avocado Pea Soup, 81
Chilled Chocolate (Dessert) Soup, 93
Forbidden Green Tea Soup, 136–137
Wasabi Avocado Whip, 153

B

Bacon bits, coconut, 208–209
Base ingredients, 10, 15
Basil
  about: benefits of, 98; as garnish, 201; other recipes with, 72, 85, 100, 120, 148, 186, 191
  Chia Pesto, 204
  Tomato-Goji Soup with Fresh Basil, 98–99
Beans and other legumes. *See also* Lentils
  about: black soybeans, 143; black superfoods, 39; buying canned, 12; canned vs. fresh, 12; cooking by type, 13; resource for, 219
  Avocado Pea Soup, 81
  Black-Eyed Pea Jambalaya, 193
  Cacao Black Bean Soup, 183
  Cauliflower-Chia Chili, 178
  Chia Tortilla Soup with Black Beans, 132–133
  Chili con Nueces, 180–181
  Coconut Curry Soup, 152
  Farmers Market Soup, 148
  Inca Chowder, 164
  Kitchari, 174–175
  Minestrone with Farrow & Chia Pesto, 140–141
  Moroccan Harira Stew, 187
  Pozole Verde with Pinto Beans, 196–197
  Red Bean Borscht, 192
  Split Pea & Hemp Seed Chowder, 157
  Summer Squash Soup with Wasabi Avocado Whip, 153
  Superfood Ramen Bowl, 142–143
  White Bean & Winter Squash Soup with Kale, 194–195
  Yogurt-Cucumber Soup with Harissa-Roasted Garbanzo Beans, 77
  Za'atar Amaranth Porridge, 169, 203
Beauty Broth, 72
Beauty, soups for. *See Soups by Benefit Index*
Beets, in Cumin Beet Soup, 118–119
Beets, in Red Bean Borscht, 192
Berries, super. *See also* Goji berries
  about: anthocyanins in, 39, 137; benefits, varieties, and uses, 26–28; camu, 26–27; cooking with, 40, 41; goldenberries, 27, 40; how to use, 28; other recipe with, 78; pomegranates, 28, 41, 126; resource for, 219; sea buckthorn, 27–28, 41; stocking, 45
  Ginger-Yam Bisque with Sea Buckthorn, 97
  Goldenberry Chutney, 212

Goldenberry Peach Gazpacho, 82–83
Persimmon Holiday Soup, 126–127
Roasted Red Pepper Soup with Sea Buckthorn Crème Fraîche, 100
Black superfoods, 39
Blenders, 17
Blending soups, 53
Bone strength, soups for. *See Soups by Benefit Index*
Bread alternatives, with soup, 215
Bread, sprouted, 147, 214
Broccoli
  about: benefits and uses, 24
  Cheesy Broccoli Soup, 159
  Coconut Curry Soup, 152
  Fritz's (Doggy) Superfood Stew, 198–199
  Many Greens Soup, 106–107
  Minestrone with Farrow & Chia Pesto, 140–141
  Pad Thai Noodle Soup, 144–145
  Roasted Broccoli Soup, 111
Broths, 56–73
  about: adding spices and salt, 61; bone broth and superfoods, 66–67; culinary, 58; freezing, 57; functional, 68; overview of, 56; in place of stocks, 57; reasons for making, 57; salt in, 61; stocks and, 57, 67; using produce "waste" for, 61; using superfood broths, 57; vegetable broth basics, 61
  Beauty Broth, 72
  Detox Broth, 71
  Energy Broth, 70
  Healing Broth, 73
  Miso Broth, 63
  Mushroom Broth, 62
  Seaweed Broth, 64
  Vegetable Broth, 60
Brothy and noodle soups, 128–155
  about: overview of, 128
  Caraway Cabbage Soup with Freekeh Balls, 134–135
  Chia Tortilla Soup with Black Beans, 132–133
  Coconut Curry Soup, 152
  Farmers Market Soup, 148
  Forbidden Green Tea Soup, 136–137
  Goji-Saffron Soup with Sorghum, 130–131
  Kimchi Dashi Bowl with Buckwheat Noodles, 146
  Minestrone with Farrow & Chia Pesto, 140–141
  Miso Noodle Soup, 138–139
  Onion Soup with Hemp Seed Parmesan, 147
  Pad Thai Noodle Soup, 144–145

ABOUT THE AUTHOR

Julie Morris is a Los Angeles-based natural food chef and advocate of whole, plant-based foods and superfoods. The bestselling author of *Superfood Smoothies* and *Superfood Kitchen*, Julie has worked in the natural food industry for close to a decade as a recipe developer, writer, cooking show host, and spokesperson, and is the executive chef for Navitas Naturals, a fair trade company that specializes in 100% organic superfoods. Her mission is simple: to share recipes and nutrition tips that make a vibrantly healthy lifestyle both easy to achieve and delicious to follow. To learn more about Julie and superfoods visit juliemorris.net.

Photo: Oliver Barth

Photographer **Oliver Barth** was born and raised in Berlin, Germany. Barth is devoted to capturing the natural beauty of life in timeless images. He lives in Los Angeles, California. Visit Oliver Barth at LAfoodphotography.com.

Photo: Steve Bonini